Biz Dev 3.0

Changing Business As We Know It

Brad Keywell

2001

ALM Publishing
New York

To get a list of resources, join the conversation, subscribe to an e-mail
newsletter about Biz Dev 3.0, please visit http://www.bizdev3.com.

Library of Congress Cataloging-in-Publication Data
Keywell, Brad, 1969-
Biz Dev 3.0: Changing Business As We Know It
Brad Keywell.
p. cm.
Includes Index.
ISBN 0-9705970-1-0
1. Electronic commerce 2.Electronic commerce-Management. I. Title.
HF5548.32.K49 2001
658—dc21   00-069971

Dedication

To the people who have filled my life with wonder,
imagination, love, and possibility...

My Mom and Dad, Stephanie and Fred

My beautiful wife, Kim

And my little angels, Chloe Isabelle
and Casey Rose

Acknowledgements

In *Letters to a Young Poet,* Ranier Maria Rilke tells us to "live the questions now. Perhaps, then, someday far in the future, you will gradually, without even noticing it, live your way into the answer." In the spirit of embracing the questions, I believe that taking the time to write is a sign of appreciation for everyone who has influenced the life experience that went into the words. Writing is also a commitment to the future, as the written word will survive us all. For any shortcomings of this book, I take full responsibility, but for its strengths I am indebted to the input and contributions of many others.

My longtime business partner, friend, and best man, Eric Lefkofsky, is at the center of my business life, and has taught me everything they did not teach in school.

Starbelly.com has been a magical experience that has shown me the best of what business can be, and has forever elevated my perception of what vision, determination and teamwork can create. To those who were a part of Starbelly, or who touched Starbelly in some way, you understand when I say that we all experienced spirituality disguised as business. To Steve Scheyer, Rick Rosenbloom, Simeon Schnapper, Rick Surkamer, RJ Segal, Jim Johnson, Matt Cohen, Renee Simpson, Dennis Huyck, Mark Giardina, and the hundreds of other motivated and dedicated technologists, artists, operators, marketers, salespeople, designers, and producers—I thought I knew what enthusiasm was, until I had the pleasure of working with you. To Pat Garrison, who creates organization out of insanity, I owe a very heartfelt thanks for always being there.

HALO is a special place, a company that feels like a family, filled with the energy and care that comes from people who are exceptional at what they do, and who take true pride in the result of their efforts. The overflowing confidence I have in the power of HALO to ever strengthen its place as the global leader of its industry comes from the spirit of each and every person who makes up the HALO family, and from knowing the quality and talent of the individuals who make up the HALO team. Special thanks to John Kelley, a true visionary, Lou Weisbach, whose support is behind HALO's every step, and Linden Nelson, a friend and advisor, who defines the meaning of persistence, and who is one of the greatest entrepreneurs I know.

Ideas are fueled by capital and great advice, and I thank many people for igniting the ideas that became the reality. Rich Heise, Steve Murray and Phil Summe of Chase Capital, and Bob Greene, Dan Malvin and Fred Wilson of Flatiron Partners saw the future and were there when we needed them, giving us truly invaluable capital—the intellectual capital of their experience and their guidance. For advice and guidance that takes many forms, but consistently challenges me to be my best, I thank, among others, Ronnie Lott, Tom Heise, Paul Reilly, Dennis Bookshester, Michael Brooks, Peter Lieberman, and Jim Zanze. Jamie Rosen is a classic entrepreneur whose creativity, ingenuity and resourcefulness I have always admired, and Andrew Sather is a visionary who has taught me more than he realizes.

I have been privileged to be in the presence of truly great educators, and I subscribe to the mantra that one of the greatest blessings a person can give another is to teach. I have been, and continue to be, touched by the intellectual foundation provided by Ben Snyder and Arlyce Seibert at Cranbrook School, Professor Herbert Barrows at the University of Michigan, and Professor J.J. White at Michigan Law School. I am lucky to be a friend of my favorite childhood author, Alfred Slote, whose creativity allowed me to experience at a young age the power of the written word. I owe special thanks to the fire that was put in my belly by Professor Fred Kiesner, now at Loyola Marymount University, who still reminds me that anything is possible if you set your mind to it.

Sincere thanks to Sam Zell, one of the world's greatest entrepreneurs, who thirteen years ago invited me into his world to experience the possibilities of capitalism and to learn from the master of the game. Sam, your plentiful advice serves as a compass for my journey, and your work, play, and philanthropic ethic is a model for all of us.

This book would not exist were it not for the hard work, dedication, and vision of several talented individuals. Jonathan Price, Joanne Cleaver, and Bob Saldeen each spent countless hours reading, rereading, and editing this work, and it owes much to their expertise and guidance. The good people at American Lawyer Media put their passion and energy into this book, and it is because of the efforts of Sara Diamond, Caroline Sorokoff, Pat Rainsford and Maggie Dalla Tana that this book came into being. I thank Seth Godin for giving both guidance and inspiration. I also acknowledge and salute all of the people profiled in the body of this text, whose "living the questions" has allowed all of us to think about the ideals of business development, and whose examples have paved the paths for many more to follow.

Finally, a special acknowledgement to my sister, Julie, who has taught me the power of family bonds, and who I deeply admire for her spirit, positive energy, persistence, and dedication to her goals. I hope I am as good a friend to her as she has been to me.

BRAD KEYWELL

Foreword

A collision is about to happen. It won't be pretty and it won't be quiet, and it will change the way you do business forever.

For years, we've been reading about how companies are becoming more interdependent. How share of mind matters as much as share of market or share of wallet. How businesses are moving faster and faster and that cooperating is far more effective than competing.

The problem comes at the last moment, when two huge ships try to dock with each other. If working with other companies is so important, how come we're so bad at it? If the future of business is all about the interrelationships we create, how on earth are we going to go about setting up those relationships? If we do it wrong, the crashes will be loud and the fallout pretty devastating.

Should we pay them? Should they pay us? How long is the deal? Should we work with them exclusively? How fast can we do this deal?

The easy way to predict the next business revolution is to look at where otherwise smart companies are wasting a ton of money. Thirty years ago, we were hemorraghing billions on robots and poor quality. Then it was the horrible waste of money that got spent on advertising. But over the last few years, the truly embarrassing flameouts have come from business development. I've watched companies waste 20 percent or 40 percent of their available cash in a single ridiculous deal with AOL. I've also seen dozens of previously great companies quietly fade away because they didn't have the guts to do the right Biz Dev deal.

At Yoyodyne, and then at Yahoo!, I got to see the worst and the best of business development. At the time, I figured that we were doomed to continue making it up as we went along, having those that followed us make the same mistakes I was watching others make. Then along came Brad.

Brad Keywell is one of the smartest, fastest, most effective entrepreneurs I've ever had the pleasure of meeting. And he's certainly among the top Biz Dev guys on the planet. Amazingly enough, Brad's decided to tell us everything he knows about the most important topic facing your company today. In simple, clear and focused prose, Keywell tells you exactly what to do ... and, most important, why.

I wish I'd read this book ten years ago.

SETH GODIN
Author, *Permission Marketing* and *Unleashing the Ideavirus*

Introduction

It's a lot like ketchup and french fries, in a strange sort of way.

For the last two years I have been immersed in a business roller-coaster ride of the most exciting kind. It started with an idea, became a business plan, grew into a venture-backed company, continued with growth from one to 230 employees in five months, resulted in a sale to the industry leader for $240 million, and ultimately led to my being named President of an NYSE company. There were two factors that were instrumental in this string of events—one I would have expected to be instrumental, the other I could never have predicted. The logical factor was people—the team that was assembled to build Starbelly.com was the best of the best, a group of people whose energy and dedication was nothing short of magical. The unexpected factor? Business development. I call it Biz Dev.

Biz Dev, while a new concept, is not a creature of the new economy. In fact, the precepts that led to its creation are as old as business itself—partnerships and alliances. The beauty of Biz Dev is that it takes the magic of partnerships and alliances and moves it to a higher ground.

Biz Dev is the semi-religious focus on reaching out to every company that can add value to your mission, and finding the most efficient touchpoint and best deal structure from which two companies can work together. This focus stems from the realization that one company can no longer be everything to everyone, and that a new recipe of partnerships and alliances must be formulated to bring the full flavor of a company's mission to bear.

If you don't believe that business development was truly instrumental in Starbelly's growth, or that it is an essential expertise to master if you want to be a leader in the future of your industry, consider a recent survey done by Forrester Research. Eighty four percent of those surveyed cited "partnerships" as the aspect of their business likely to grow in the next year, far exceeding technology, personnel, or new product offerings. Biz Dev encompasses partnerships, alliances, and a mosaic of deals that allow two companies to work together while not merging or buying each other. Biz Dev, as this book illustrates, is the competency that tips the competitive scale. It's worthy of your attention (and passion) because you should be making it tip the scale in your direction, and harnessing it to be a cornerstone of your future success.

So what's the story with the ketchup and french fries, you might ask?

Biz Dev has become, without a lot of attention, one of the conceptual pillars supporting our business landscape. You may be unaware of its significance, and may even take it for granted. Most business concepts—direct marketing, cost accounting, direct sales—start small, spread through sporadic trial, get explored by leading business schools, are developed into theories, and after tens of years become accepted tenets of successfully doing business. Biz Dev, on the other hand, just happened.

Biz Dev is now so ingrained in the mindsets of the most effective entrepreneurs and companies that it is almost like ketchup and french fries. You take it for granted that ketchup goes with fries, so you rarely stop to consider that there was once no such union. To those in business today, the Biz Dev discipline is part of business itself, as inseparable as our friend the fry and his buddy ketchup.

All of this may have you wondering why a book would be written about how to be successful at Biz Dev, if the concept is such a fixture in today's business landscape. Well, the fact is that while those of us who live Biz Dev believe it to be as important as other functions like sales and marketing, some do not agree. Why? Because they have not been exposed to Biz Dev, and therefore may not know what it is, or may not grasp how dynamically it changes business as we know it.

If you don't really "get" what Biz Dev is, or if Biz Dev is so much a part of your life that you can't believe that anyone does not recognize its importance for a successful business, consider the following. Business schools still do not teach business development. Corporate titles such as Vice President of Business Development are new to the lingo of business. Companies invest hundreds of millions, even billions, in sales and marketing, and can quantify for you the commensurate return on investment, hit rates, coverage ratios, and reams of other data, yet few could either quantify or qualify their investment in or their return on Biz Dev. At the same time, the words "Business Development" show up significantly more often than "Venture Capital" or "Mergers and Acquisitions" in a recent LEXIS/NEXIS database search.

At Starbelly, the leading Internet-based promotional products company that is now a part of HALO Industries, the world's largest promotional products company, Biz Dev meant exploring partnerships and alliances with procurement portals, art licensors, television and movie studios, bricks-and-mortar companies in the promotional products industry, software providers, franchise printing chains, major universities, rock bands, industry associations, search engines, marketing cooperatives, and Fortune 1000 companies, just to name a few. Our passionate team has spoken at hundreds of conferences and we have been in thousands of face-to-face meetings exploring possible Biz Dev opportunities. We have been unrelenting in our mission, exploring every possible opportunity to create value for our business by sharing value with other businesses through partnerships and alliances.

Before I send you off on your way to read *Biz Dev 3.0*, and see if you "get it," I want to make a simple prediction. The Biz Dev principles outlined in this book will form the nucleus for a recognized and accepted part of every business in the next decade. Biz Dev "experts" will come out of the woodwork in every field and every industry. Biz Dev teams will find their place in the offices and boardrooms of every business in America, and will prove their importance in the generation of revenues, profits, and market share. Biz Dev will be acknowledged as a cost-effective way to achieve business goals, and will be one of the primary differentiators between good companies and great companies.

It's time to take Biz Dev seriously and to analyze this crucial business discipline. It's time to realize that Biz Dev has become the competitive advantage, and that if you do not become good at it, your competitor will. Once you understand the process you will be able to appreciate the underinvestment in it (and the overinvestment in areas such as sales and marketing), and the impact you can have on both your top and bottom line by making yourself and your company the best in your industry at Biz Dev.

You may not accept my prediction, and you may be skeptical of my enthusiasm for the importance of business development. If so, you are the person for whom I've written this book. You are the reason I've gone to such great lengths to document not only the role of Biz Dev, but the practicioners who have proven what good (and bad) Biz Dev looks like. It is for you that I've illustrated not only why this concept may have evaded you up until now, but also why it will be critical to your future.

As Ferris Bueller once said, "Life moves pretty fast. If you don't stop and look around once in a while, you could miss it." I hope you stop to look around this book, and I hope it leaves you better prepared for your future.

BRAD KEYWELL
Chicago, Illinois

Contents

Step 2: Find allies everywhere 69

Step 3: Speed + simplicity = success 101

Step 4: Customers connect the dots 133

Step 5: Negotiate without baggage   149

Step 6: Deliver more than the deal   169

Step 7: Grow it or kill it   189

Opening up Biz Dev

You probably don't think you have time to read this book. In fact, I didn't think I had time to write it—until I realized how important the evolved discipline of Business Development is to the current landscape of business. So, if you're really too busy to read this book, here are the main points:

- Your business is really about **developing relationships**, not products, services, or things.

- You can **spot potential allies everywhere**—if you just take your customer's point of view.

- You must **move faster** than ever before, so your deals have to be simpler.

- Your customers are the ones driving you to **form alliances**. You make partners to serve and preserve your customers.

- You must **leave the baggage** of old-style legal wrangling outside when you go into the room to work out a deal. Get ready to **improvise**.

- Your whole company has to **get behind the deals** you make—or growth stops.

Biz Dev jet-fuels the merging of the old and new economies—producing the E-conomy. Biz Dev has been at the core of the economy's transformation. **Biz Dev lets you accelerate any business.**

Why is Biz Dev so powerful? It combines the speed of the new economy with the discipline of the old economy, transforming the potential of what every business can become. It allows each of us to change the future of our businesses—forever—through innovative partnerships and alliances. It provides the ability to replace "competition" with "co-opetition."

Anyone—even you—can get into the Biz Dev mindset, but first you have to rethink your business.

Biz Dev happens at Internet speed, but make no mistake—it is not the same thing as the Internet. The speed of Biz Dev is the speed of creativity and innovation on steroids. It's the speed of conceiving of a different playing field for your future, and instantaneously growing the grass, building the stands, painting the lines, and lining up to play. Biz Dev represents a completely new idea about how growth happens.

No matter what industry you're in, Biz Dev is now the single best way to build your business. So here's the boring but scholarly way of framing what we're talking about:

Biz Dev is the process of rapidly growing a business by partnering with other companies in order to penetrate a market that would be otherwise unattainable.

A company partners with another that has a specialty it needs, but would take too long, or demand too many resources, to acquire on its own.

Why do I call this book *Biz Dev 3.0*? Because I've been through first-hand experience learning how to do Biz Dev from scratch (Version 1), and I've gone through the trial-and-error necessary to understand what it is, how it works, and how it doesn't work (sort of the "get out the bugs" phase, which we'll call Version 2), and what I'm giving you now really works (hence, Version 3.0).

Biz Dev is less than ten years old, but already it's been proven.

- It started in Silicon Valley, where everyone knows each other and there are entire ecosystems of particular industries growing.

- It spread through the Internet.
- Now it's attracting major brick-and-mortar, blue-chip companies that used to define themselves around big, bulky stuff like power plants, cars on the lot, or natural gas.

I got into Biz Dev because I had to. My partner and I had a vision of the future of an industry, and the only way to make that real was to engage in a process that we would later learn was the essence of Biz Dev.

- Our business is promotional products.
- Our concept was to revolutionize it by setting up brand stores within other companies' Web sites.
- Our method was to talk to everyone, throw out every notion of confidentiality, and let passion and persistence be our guide.

The result? The business that we started, Starbelly.com, was acquired for $240 million by HALO Industries (the largest company in our industry) and I became President of HALO, a New York Stock Exchange publically traded company.

So I've seen Biz Dev from the inside, and I've tracked some of the biggest practitioners of this new art.

My point of view comes out of my own experience, but the facts come from all over the E-conomy.

These days, alliances **dominate** the business news. According to Survdata, alliances were mentioned 2,926 times in news releases in the first quarter of 2000, beating out venture capitalists and investments (2,414 mentions), mergers (1,292 mentions), and IPOs (1,226 mentions). Surprised, huh? I was too, but I hope that by the time you finish this book you'll realize that alliances and partnerships are the true wealth creators of this E-conomy. Forget individual wealth creation—Biz Dev creates massive wealth for the companies and industries involved. **Biz Dev is *the* hidden essence of the strength of new business growth in the last five years.**

If you line up two companies side by side and one of them has a robust Biz Dev effort aggressively pushing alliances and partnerships, and the other firm doesn't, you'll see **a measurable difference in the valuation (and consumer acceptance)** of those firms. Why? Because the more allies and partners you have, the more relevant you become to your customers, and the more essential you become to the landscape and value chain of your industry.

The *Industry Standard* runs a column every week about deals, partnerships and alliances—and the dozen or so that might be important enough to get into its column are only a tiny fraction of the number of deals that were actually announced that week. For the first time, alliances and partnerships have become a **metric** by which a company is judged.

Biz Dev Buzz: These days, Business Development is a **requirement**, not an option.

Source: NEXIS search for "business development."

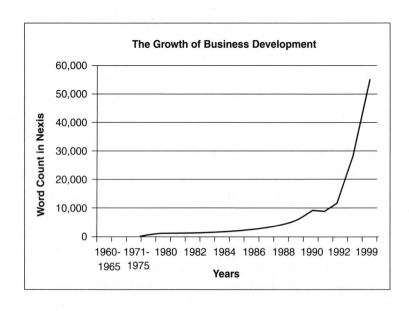

The uncorked secret of Biz Dev

At its heart, Biz Dev is a giant "virtual" cocktail party, attended by companies (not people), at which these companies mill about, introduce themselves to each other, and find out what they have in common. Once the connections are made, the companies follow up to harness the elements that they have in common to create value. But how do you get to that cocktail party?

In Silicon Valley in the early 1990s all the companies were close to each other, and people jumped from one to another, so there were wide-ranging alumni networks from which instant partnerships could spring. If you aren't already enmeshed in such an ecosystem, you'll need to reach out and find potential partners.

As a first step, join our ongoing conversation at the Biz Dev 3.0 Web site, at **http://www.BizDev3.com**. You'll be able to compare notes with other folks who think Biz Dev is a fantastic and exciting way to grow a business. You'll see what's new, and what's not, in Biz Dev, and soon you'll be able to help newbies along.

The great virtual cocktail party

Once Biz Dev is on your mind, you'll start to realize it's happening all around you.

Biz Dev became the *lingua franca* of the new economy, the common language of dot-coms, high-tech infrastructure firms, and the leading technology companies, because these companies needed this discipline in order to grow. To stake their claim as innovators, they had to reach out to other companies and find innovative ways to create value together.

Then the old-economy companies, seeing that their lunches were getting devoured by dot-coms, got Biz Dev religion, too.

With the new economy and old economy now merging into one big E-conomy, Biz Dev is the newly proven essence of growing a business.

- It works for **any company**, of any size, in any industry.
- It works if you do it a little, but works better if you do it **a lot**.
- It's not sales, or marketing, or mergers and acquisitions, though it does include elements of **all of those** disciplines.

Biz Dev is a completely fresh approach to building your company. By the time you flip the last page of this book, you'll know exactly how you can leverage your company's strengths with the strengths of other companies to create entirely new products that hit the market at the right time, through the right channels, to bring in new customers, revenues and profits.

By touching each other at a specific point with the aim of reaching a particular market in a particular way, and then going right ahead and making the partnership happen, companies are redefining the nature and importance of relationships as an essential part of growing the business.

Biz Dev means a complete recalibration of how businesses grow. That's why I realized that nothing can be more important than taking the time to tell you what I and the rest of the

Starbelly.com team have learned as we've figured out the dynamics and rules of Biz Dev.

From the first week we launched Starbelly, we have held regular meetings at which everyone in the company swaps stories about business development, new relationships, and tales from the Internet front. We're all in this together.

This is your invitation to be part of this ongoing conversation—a virtual member of our **Starbelly Sessions**—and to meet entrepreneurs around the country, as we all learn about this new way to expand our businesses.

Do you feel lost?

For a while now, you may have had a sense that something was changing. Who were all these people titled Vice President of Business Development? What's up with all these announcements of alliances, partnerships, joint-product introductions and blended distribution deals?

Do you get the feeling that you really ought to have lots of other companies' logos on your own company's Web site—even though you're not sure what that would do for you?

Why do articles in all those fat Internet business magazines constantly toss off comments about alliances and 'doing deals' and how the Business Development honcho pulled off a miracle—without ever slowing down to define what business development actually is and what the honcho does with it?

Biz Dev is still a surprise to many people exactly because it *wasn't* taught in business school.

Biz Dev has burst on the scene too quickly for academics to have researched it. It's moving too fast for very many consultants to have latched onto it as a new line of work.

Those who are doing Biz Dev are on the run, and they're bringing many others in their companies along for the ride. The rest of us, who grew up in the traditional economy and are used to the research/marketing/sales cycle, are left wondering, "Hey, what are they doing different? And can I get in on this, too?"

If you've been wondering about questions like these, you've got plenty of company.

Many smart business people ignored Biz Dev when it got rolling in the early 1990s and, by the late 1990s, these folks started to find themselves outflanked by competitors. Even though its own Technology Research group cited business-to-business collaboration as one of the hottest technology and Internet company trends back in January 2000, one investment banking firm didn't announce its first partnership until June 2000.

The technology division of consulting firm Renaissance Worldwide aggressively cut partnership deals with e-commerce leaders like CommerceOne for two years before the parent company caught on to the power of Biz Dev. It wasn't until January 2000 that Renaissance Worldwide finally made its first sales and marketing alliance. In June 2000, Renaissance stock was scraping bottom at $1.50 per share. The point is that this is new to everyone—which presents an opportunity. If you get ahead of the curve on Biz Dev, you win!

You're never too big for Biz Dev

Take a close look at SAP AG, the German software giant.

In the mid 1990s, SAP and Peoplesoft were in a wrestling match to convert every single company on the planet to their enterprise software systems. Both companies had the same vision—to convert all of a company's back-room operations, from manufacturing line to accounting to shipping, to one seamless computer platform.

Great idea—but while SAP was occupied with trying to throttle Peoplesoft, the Internet happened.

All of a sudden, the attention of big company CIOs was drawn away by the vision of communicating transparently with the outside world—not smoothing out turf battles between the front office and the guys on the shipping dock.

SAP was very slow to wake up to the fact that it had to reorient its mammoth software systems to be outwardly focused, and not preoccupied with purely inner workings. Throughout 1998, its programmers labored to write mySAP, which was introduced in mid-1999. mySAP enables users to organize the information they need from the Internet, and from within their companies, in a single desktop browser. Great idea. Too bad it was too late.

In May 2000, SAP announced that it was going to spend $1 billion in the coming twelve months to partner with Internet software companies. It bought part of Industry-to-Industry, Inc.

Hasso Plattner, co-chief executive, told the *Wall St. Journal* that "The facets of applications have exploded. The universe of technology is too big for one company." This, from a company that previously **dominated** its space, a company that once envisioned itself as being everything to everyone.

Scared yet? You should be.

These are smart companies with **world-wide influence.** But they can't compete by themselves. The rate of change is too fast for them to see every opportunity with huge potential.

With Biz Dev partners, they will have an extra army scouting out field intelligence, the better to leverage relationships to pounce on emerging business trends. They will have a new way of seeing things so they can take new ground in their markets, not just try to protect what they already have.

It is almost impossible for a single company to put all facets of commerce, technology, distribution and marketing together, on its own, in a time frame that will deliver success.

Biz Dev rewrites the rules

The deluge of co-operative marketplace, distribution and marketing deals announced in the late 1990s and in the new millenium shows how many old-line industrials have finally seen the light. Partnerships and alliances are the mileposts of the new business landscape.

The future's only going to bring more of these deals. And if those guys—with every technological resource at their disposal—didn't get it at first, what chance do the little and mid-sized companies have?

A huge chance! **The little guys can finally play on a level playing field with the big guys—if the little guys exploit Biz Dev.**

Biz Dev is a **fantastic equalizer.** When small companies and start-ups forge meaningful, market-specific alliances and partnerships with larger companies, the competition is suddenly faced with a serious threat.

You can brush away a gnat, but a swarm of gnats is hard to ignore. Small companies that surround themselves with well-chosen partners are able to increase their market presence geometrically—even exponentially.

Think about it:

- Technology companies like Quicken.com, Blue Martini, and Ariba have become **essential to their spaces through their network of partnerships**, even though much larger companies like Microsoft arguably could and should have beaten them to the punch.
- Verisign, Network Solutions, and Checkfree have become essential tools for the new economy, beating out much larger logical competitors, due to their Biz Dev powers.
- Cisco is continually acquiring young start-ups who have proven they can beat Cisco at parts of its own game, even though Cisco itself is most logically equipped to dominate its entire industry.

Biz Dev Buzz: Biz Dev is the agility that all small and young companies need to embrace in order to become giant killers.

An evolution of Biz Dev

In the middle of 1999, Starbelly.com was founded, and a Biz Dev journey began. We had a vision of a better way for an industry to operate. The industry is promotional products—in other words, stuff with corporate logos on it (like golf shirts, mugs, umbrellas, and anything else that can be imprinted with a logo).

This industry is huge, estimated to be larger than $15 billion annually, yet the industry is extremely fragmented. You have an enormous number of sales people (more than 18,000 companies) calling on a huge customer base (we estimate that nearly every company in America buys stuff imprinted with their logos on it), and an equally large supplier base (more than 21,000 suppliers who make the stuff with the logos on it).

The Starbelly vision was to use the Internet to create **a better business model**. The traditional role of the salesperson as "order taker" would be transformed into someone who would make the sale, and then have the "tools" of the Internet to allow the customer to re-order automatically, to provide the customer "virtual" company stores on the Internet or on his or her own intranet, and to link the Starbelly ordering system into the customer's internal procurement system. In other words, don't replace the salesperson—rather, glorify him. Make the salesperson a resource to an entire portfolio of value-added tools.

On the supply chain side, our vision was to link all of the fragmented players in the supply chain (the people who make the shirts and the golf balls, the people who imprint on the golf balls, the people who embroider on the shirts, the people who ship the stuff from point-to-point, and everyone else in between), and connect them over the Internet with a common "language," which would result in a real-time tracking system showing exactly where all the products are all the time. In other words, the same functionality of FedEx (allowing you to punch in a tracking number and see exactly where that package is), translated into our industry. This vision was one that would **change the industry**, adding huge efficiencies and tremendously better customer interfaces.

Great idea. But in order to make it real, and to attempt to affect an industry, **it had to come together fast**. Real fast. Good ideas are only worth as much as the execution behind them, and an idea this logical would surely have competitors.

Our determination to turn this vision into reality was intense, but the old methods of negotiation and linear business growth would not serve it well. This new company, Starbelly, had to figure out how to move quicker and more effectively than any of the Starbelly team members had ever done in their previous jobs. We had to create an environment of speed, traction, and effectiveness, or else our vision would be in jeopardy of being one of the many "good idea, but never happened" stories. If we could create instant acceptance and recognition of our new way to operate in our industry, we believed the rest would take care of itself.

We're smart, but other people are too. We knew that our idea could easily be snagged by someone else, totally independently.

No one else was doing anything close to what we had in mind, so we couldn't buy our way into the market.

Our core team sat down together in a small Chicago neighborhood bar and we hashed out the plan over beer. We would have to grow by networking with other companies that already had the expertise, market credibility, and clout to get us the technical expertise, marketing savvy, and open doors that we needed. We couldn't buy, we didn't have time to build. Biz Dev was **the only way**.

We realized that we needed all the help we could get. We were able to collaborate with other companies on a scale that I'd never thought about before. Our experience blew the lid off my old ideas about linear business growth, just as this book will for you.

Suddenly every other company seemed potentially valuable to us. We had the power to reach into its operations and talk directly with its employees and collaborate with them quickly, efficiently and immediately. Together, we were able to find out how to help our mutual customers.

As we brought in investors, explained our plan to suppliers, hired technological experts, and started persuading customers of the wisdom of the Starbelly approach, we also invited them to drop in on our weekly beer and business bull sessions.

Soon, anywhere from 100 to 300 people were jammed into each Starbelly session at the Morseland, that small neighborhood bar.

We passed around a microphone, and anyone who had something great to add, added it. It could be the announcement of a new deal or a piece of news about the market, or some customer feedback. And now you're listening in on our sessions, too. Once you get the feel of Biz Dev, I hope you'll weigh in with your thoughts and stories, at our Biz Dev 3 site, at **http://www.BizDev3.com**.

Sessions like these let everyone pick up tips and ideas from other folks, and figure out what was working, and why. In a way, this book is a summary of those discussions.

Growth Timeline for Starbelly.com

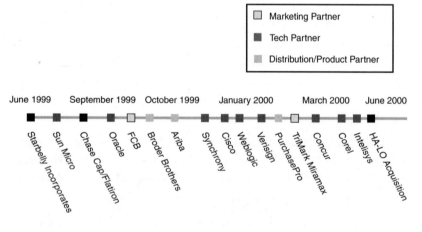

Growth Timeline: Progression of Business Development at Starbelly.com

The fast track—the only track

Technology is changing too quickly for any one company to master every new tool, every new program, every new interface that will help it communicate quickly and smoothly with its customers.

It's hard enough to integrate new technology that you develop in conjunction with technology partners—how could any company hand-construct it all in-house, in a short time frame? That's impossible.

Through Biz Dev, you can get the technology you need, better built and faster built, so you can get your products out there in the market ahead of the clueless competition. Ditto for distribution, operations and marketing.

Other companies have ways to reach markets you wish *you* had. **You *can* have that market access—through Biz Dev partnerships.**

Operational finesse and efficiency can be yours—through Biz Dev.

Marketing insights, smart strategies and clever tactics—yours through Biz Dev.

In the past, companies could afford the time to perfect products internally, then methodically work through a predictable progression of prototypes, focus groups and test markets before going live with the new products. Other companies followed the same procedures. Everyone was **slow** together. (How quaint—everyone moving so slow that no one had any conception of what *fast* could look like.)

Even software was rolled out in waves: 1.0, 1.5, 2.0 and so on. Only customers who were willing to live on the bleeding edge of technology bought 1.0. Who wanted to suffer through all the bugs and glitches and crashes? Not the general business public. Most people only considered buying at 2.0.

The Internet changed all that. To grab market share, awareness and a solid foothold in the hundreds of new markets that sprang into being between 1996 and 1998, thousands of companies realized that they didn't have the luxury of obsessing over every detail before going public. Wait, and you would watch others claim prime categories for their own. Boldly announce that you were the 'market leader' and let the others try to prove that you weren't.

Suddenly, the tables were turned.

Slow and secret left you high and dry. Sure, you finally came out with your perfect product—but by then, who cared?

Companies that were quick and loud had already attracted most of the attention. Sure, their products were still in development, but they harnessed the strengths of other companies for technology, distribution, operations and marketing.

Suddenly, the market had tolerance for 'in process.'

Done trumped perfection.

Biz Dev Buzz: If you try to build from scratch, you'll still be arguing with the contractor over where to dig the basement while your Biz-Dev-powered competition is lounging in its new family room.

The Internet launched Biz Dev

Internet companies were the first ones to use Biz Dev as the main way to grow. They had to, because they were being pushed along by their technology to get much bigger, faster, than companies before them.

Just to keep their heads above water, Internet companies had to find new ways of getting the resources they needed, first to become operational companies, and then to keep pushing ahead in the market.

So instead of growing all the expertise and resources and market contacts they'd need from inside, they developed close partnerships and alliances with other companies.

They all **borrowed** from each other, and the ones who were best at maximizing that borrowed strength were the ones who got the fastest start, and who are still going strongest.

The rush to embrace the Internet also broke through the traditional hesitation to embrace the '1.0' version of anything. The entire Internet was '1.0.' Everyone was in it together. Everyone realized that they couldn't afford to wait for the '2.0' version of anything.

One of the main assets that traditional companies get when they buy Internet upstarts is the **constellation of relationships**—the huge number of functioning partnerships that help an upstart make enough waves to become an attractive acquisition target. When traditional companies value Internet companies, one of the things they look at is the way the takeover target has added value to its core mission by drawing in partners through Biz Dev. The more impressive the partners and the more effective and fruitful the results of the marketing, operations and distribution alliances, the more value there is for the traditional company to buy.

The third way

Businesses don't grow just from the inside or the outside. There's a new, **third way.**

Those of us who have grown up with the traditional linear business growth models find this shift frightening. And we should.

We can't count on our new ideas being put in a queue for consideration, analysis, research and approval or rejection by the marketing department. We can't count on our suppliers behaving the way they used to. They might start going around us directly to the end market. Carefully nurtured, crafted, and protected exclusive partnerships now appear to strangle growth, not encourage it. We can't count on the fact that our competitors are going to take just as long to get a new product to market as we do, giving us a comfortable margin for error. We can no longer test and refine a product into perfection before we introduce it.

This shift is disorienting—as if we've been driving along a highway across the plains and we suddenly run into a spaghetti bowl of intersections, interchanges, merging lanes and off-ramps. Straight ahead, left and right aren't the only options any more.

Who knows which exit will lead to a blind alley and which will prove to be a shortcut that gets you to your destination hours early, calm and relaxed? And as you continue driving, the road rises up only about 100 feet in front of your car. You never know when a new exit will suddenly appear, leaving you only seconds to decide whether to take it or pass it by.

Traditionally structured business relationships may still deliver the positioning and products you want for your company—but they may cripple you too. You may find yourself looking for synergies in places you used to ignore—competitors, start-up vendors, people within your company who used to be of most value channeling their ideas and energy in a straight line within their departments. Looking for someone to blame? Kick the Internet.

Shock therapy for the old economy

I hope you've already said goodbye to the old economy, because it's long gone.

The Internet—the most remarkable communications and information tool known to man—has changed even the stodgiest old companies. No matter how resistant an industry is, how in love a business may be with its current technology, or how illogical a Web play might seem on the surface, Biz Dev is popping up in the most unlikely places. Biz Dev acts as an accelerant to Web-based businesses even in grease-and-gear industries.

- **TruckersB2B.com** is a Web site formed to provide meaningful cost savings to trucking companies. It's owned by one of America's top ten truckload carriers, GE Capital, and several other leading financial institutions. Truckers! That's as old-economy as you can get. But this co-op promises to draw together a multitude of resources that can help truckers with all the services that surround the effort of getting the big rig on the road, from roadside servicing to finding the right parts and leasing.

- **Airline consortia.** Upset at the runaway success enjoyed by Priceline.com (the name-your-price company that was wholly created through very imaginative Biz Dev partnerships), the airlines fought back. Their tool of choice: Biz Dev. Several global coalitions of airlines such as Orbitz are aiming to shoot Priceline.com from the sky by offering their own copycat name-your-price services, along with a wide array of other ways to get tickets. Sure, they've all participated in joint reservations systems before, but that was purely a back-room efficiency play. The new consortia are designed to create a brand awareness of their own; founders are already lining up the marketing alliances.

- **Streamline.com** partners with a wide variety of companies to position itself as the ultimate household helper. Through Streamline, customers can ship packages via UPS; they can leave clothes for dry-cleaning and shoes for repair; they can get bottled water delivered. Even local charities benefit when Streamline picks up donations left for them. Streamline's partners include traditional companies like food, drug and pet supply manufacturers, as well as other dot-coms, such as Proflowers.com and Nordstrom.com.

- **WebCaskets.com** ("click here for live help") has partnered with casket makers, monument and marker companies, and florists to launch a national service for the most local of services—funerals and burials. National funeral home chains work hard to keep a small-town image as they acquire family-owned chains. The traditional thinking in the industry is that grieving relatives value trust over price. But here's Webcaskets with its cheery logo turning that assumption on its head and winning customers by promoting practicality and price over emotion. It recreated in a matter of months the partner networks that the funeral home chains have been protecting for decades.

Pick up a copy of the *Industry Standard* (the weekly news magazine that covers e-commerce trends) and tally up the number of ads that prominently display partners' logos along with that of the company actually advertising. In one recent issue, I found that, of the first twenty full-page ads, sixteen of the advertising companies displayed their partners' logos on their Web sites; four of the companies mentioned their partners in their print ads; and of the four companies that didn't mention their partners, three were old economy.

You can take any business idea, any one at all, and jet-fuel it through Biz Dev. A Biz Dev mindset will allow you to make it happen quicker, and will prompt you to find allies to ensure the idea's success.

No matter what business you're in, or how old that business is, or stuck in its ways, or even how boring and barely profitable it is, you can use Biz Dev to transform it completely.

You'll beat your competitors, but maybe even more important, you'll be having fun. Your imagination will get a workout as you start to see connections between your company and others, that you've never seen before. You'll get energized as you see how much your creativity helps your customers. You might even get a little rich along the way.

Biz Dev Buzz: Every company can benefit in some way from Biz Dev. There are no dead ends.

How did I miss this in B School?

Until a few years ago, the articulated concept of Biz Dev didn't really exist.

It still doesn't—not in syllabi and curricula, anyway.

Students today aren't being taught case studies in the history of Biz Dev because it has evolved much too quickly. Biz Dev has grown up without being taught, driven by thousands of individual companies that wanted to seize opportunities. People do Biz Dev, and have not yet taken the time to give hour-long lectures about it. Biz Dev is characterized by speed and action—two traits **rarely found** in business schools.

B schools are just beginning to add courses about e-commerce. Maybe Biz Dev is next. But first, they have to figure out where Biz Dev fits—and it really doesn't fit neatly into the departments of marketing and so on. Negotiation, sales skills, market research, operations and marketing all play into Biz Dev, but none of them defines it. Where does Biz Dev fit in the B school organization chart? I don't know.

That's their problem, not yours. You're faced with **market realities** right now. You have ideas that will take way too long to get off the ground unless you tap into the expertise of already existing companies. You have channels and operations and technologies that you want to leverage to blanket your market—right now.

We're all in the soup together, figuring out new ways to use Biz Dev. You could say we are getting our MBAs from the School of Hard Clicks. When you're done reading this book you'll have more than an intellectual understanding of what Biz Dev is all about—you'll also have an intuitive sense of what makes one deal great and another stink so bad it should be taken out with that day's garbage. When you put down this book, I hope you'll be able to pick up a copy of the *Wall St. Journal* or the *Industry Standard* and read a story about a new partnership or alliance and know, immediately, "This makes sense" or ask yourself, "What are these two companies thinking?"

Biz Dev is **an ongoing conversation**. We'll learn it from you, just as we learned the basics from the partners that helped us convert Starbelly from an idea to a real business.

What we at Starbelly learned about business development can help you, and what you learn will loop back to help us. There are no six degrees of separation in Biz Dev. There's only one degree—the link between us—and the more we know about how to push this new way of doing business to the max, the faster and better all of our companies will run. The faster and better our partners run, the quicker and more on target we can be when we serve our customers. Deeper, richer, more profitable customer satisfaction is the ultimate validation of Biz Dev. Because that's the goal, customers have the most to teach us about Biz Dev.

Biz Dev Buzz: No one has a corner on Biz Dev wisdom.

Even the U.S. government realizes that the Internet is already interwoven into the fabric of the economy. In 1998, the feds called their report on the economic impact of computers and the Internet *The Emerging Digital Economy*. The latest version of the report, which landed in June 2000, was simply called *The Digital Economy* "because it's here. In fact, it has become the driving force of the American Economy," said Secretary of Commerce William M. Daley. Real investment in information technology doubled between 1995 and 1999, from $243 billion to $510 billion.

—Source: U.S. Department of Commerce

Spotting Biz Dev B.S.

If you think I'm suggesting that all Biz Dev is good Biz Dev, think again. There are plenty of pitfalls that distinguish effective Biz Dev from a waste of time. Here are ten to consider:

1. If someone says that he's been in Biz Dev for more than five or six years, he's probably lying, unless he started with a high-tech powerhouse like Cisco, Oracle, or a very early Internet company.

2. Anyone who says that she's been in Biz Dev "all my life" is just applying a bit of Post-It surgery to the resume. The most progressive companies didn't start thinking this way until 1994.

3. Real Biz Dev experts talk **deals, not sales.**

4. Real Biz Dev experts talk about **market value** added to their companies, not quarterly profits and losses.

5. Real Biz Dev uses a Rolodex like a rifle, not a shotgun.

6. Real Biz Dev experts have the persistence of a pit bull and the persuasive powers of Oprah to get people inside their companies on their side, and to get those outside their companies to see the **mutual advantage** in a proposed deal.

7. Real Biz Dev keeps out lawyers, accountants, investment bankers, and other nitpickers. Too much analysis on the front-end of a partnership can kill.

8. Real Biz Dev focuses on the people who will **create the value added**, not on the physical assets, the distribution chain, or anything that's on an organizational chart.

9. Cowboys need not apply. Real Biz Dev **involves teams** on both sides who instantly get the vision and become evangelists for it, drawing in the resources to make it happen.

10. Speed is a perishable asset. **Keep up, or get out.**

What you think you know (aka "The Old Way")

1. Your company's stuff is always better than anything your competitors come up with.

2. If your stuff isn't better, you're working on it, and the market knows that what you guys make is worth waiting for.

3. Your company's track record is so good that customers will wait to see what you'll come out with, out of curiosity and out of loyalty.

4. Your competitors **have** to pay attention to your company because it is what it is.

5. The more stuff your company owns, the more powerful it is. That stuff can be processes, services, or people.

6. Other companies want to find out what's going on in yours, and you can bet they'll stab you in the back with whatever they dig up.

7. Your suppliers have already stuck with you through thick and thin, and they'll keep on sticking.

8. But your suppliers absolutely do not want the messiness and hassle of dealing with end users and customers.

9. You've got a nice, cushy rut in the supply chain. You earned it, it's yours, and you're not gonna give it up.

10. First, prove to me that change is worth it. Prove to me that scrapping the cushy rut and breaking up links in the supply chain is going to deliver more money and more customers. Then I'll think about changing.

11. Push the envelope, get a paper cut.

12. A conversation at the country club is the best way to get new business.

13. We go back a long way. Hey, we're family! Practically.

What you must know now (Reality check)

1. Your stuff might be better than everyone else's in your market. It might be mediocre. It might stink.

2. Nobody cares about what you might do. That doesn't help them today. While you've got your head stuck in a lab, or a report, or you're perfecting something into irrelevance, your competitors are picking off your best customers.

3. Your history isn't worth the cassette tape it's recorded on.

4. You're known by the company you keep. So who is your company hanging out with now?

5. Are your competitors staying awake at night worrying about what you're up to? If you don't think they are, you should worry about what they're up to.

6. Show and tell. The more people who know what you're doing, how you're developing your market, where you're going and how you're getting there, the greater the chances that you'll link up with someone who can help you get there.

7. Your suppliers don't give a rip about where you've been. They want to know where you're going.

8. Your suppliers want to get into bed with the end users.

9. Behind your back, others in your supply chain are wondering what it is, exactly, that you bring to the party.

10. Suck it up. The change is relentless. It will only get faster. It will only look messier. Get used to being surprised.

11. Get a paper cut. Put on a band-aid.

12. Who has time for a country club?

13. Right. Well, you can't choose your family, but you can choose your business relationships.

No risk, no reward

Better safe than sorry?

No.

Better sorry than safe.

Staying safe will probably make you sorry anyway. These days, there's more risk in standing still or moving slowly than there is in moving quickly and expecting to make changes along the way. **If this idea of Biz Dev seems risky to you, then, good.** You'll really think through all the ways that your company needs to be open to other companies.

If you're afraid that your business relationships won't stand up to the strain of sharing your plans and projects, then, good. You'll figure out how to find partners you can trust to keep your best interests in mind along with theirs.

If you're afraid that your company can't move fast enough to take advantage of all the intersections of opportunity and ability to serve mutual markets that you have with other companies, then, good. You'll be the one hammering on the president's door, asking for the authority to tap into other departments within your company to get the authority and people to make those deals happen before they evaporate.

As you get comfortable with Biz Dev, you'll start to see deals, partnerships and alliances **everywhere you go.** After you've had a few successes that help your company as much as your partners, you'll start to win converts inside your company. And as you get those successes, if you don't start to get respect for Biz Dev from others, I suggest you look for another job.

Biz Dev recruiters want to know first and foremost about the deals you've negotiated—what outside companies you brought in as partners, for what purpose, and with what results. A recruiter can take your under-appreciated performance and flip it into a better job at a company that wants to be a Biz Dev powerhouse, probably for more money and some options, too.

I can hear you thinking: sure, Biz Dev is important for start-up companies and small companies. It's all upside for them. They get reflected glory from a bigger company. But what does the bigger company get? It already has loads of customers and suppliers, plus, probably, brand awareness that it has worked hard and spent millions of dollars to create.

Absolutely. Start-ups and dot-coms are asking established companies to take the risk of letting unproven partners trade on their reputations.

What do the big companies get from Biz Dev? Just a few things—fresh ideas, new talents, perspectives on the market they'd never have gotten any other way—oh—and a bit of credibility in the fastest-growing market segments.

Biz Dev is completely **a two-way street**. Small start-ups with brilliant ideas and aggressive talent bring the cachet of cutting-edge market awareness to big companies. Ocean liners get into port by using tugboats to guide them up to the dock. Sometimes, they can only get that particular dock by pairing up with a smaller company that is nimble and focused enough to bring them to the exact spot where people are eagerly awaiting the cargo that the ocean liner carries.

Biz Dev Buzz: To be effective, Biz Dev must move in every direction—inside the company and outside.

Try it, you'll like it

Growing a business is exhilarating. There's no better, faster way to get this buzz than through creative, focused Biz Dev. You'll expand your professional horizons, meet new people and realize potential that may not have had a place to go before.

Plus, it's **fun**. The exhilaration of growing Starbelly from scratch, and executing on a business model to make our industry more efficient, has been great. What could be more rewarding—professionally and personally —than working with others to serve the market in imaginative ways that get people's attention, loyalty and passion?

Biz Dev is touch and go. We're alert to detect changes and respond immediately. We're assuming that the situation could change abruptly and we must monitor it carefully.

Pilots are required by the Federal Aviation Administration to keep their skills fresh by completing a certain number of landings and takeoffs in a given period of time. Beginning pilots have to stop completely, taxi back to the end of the runway, and then take off again. But experienced pilots can condense their takeoff/landing cycle by "touch and go"—landing and then immediately forcing the plane to prepare for another takeoff, within seconds. That's how they make sure that they've fulfilled the FAA's requirements in the shortest amount of time.

The parallel for business development is that you can never come to a full stop, get back into position and then taxi for another takeoff. Today's markets are too demanding. In order to see what opportunities lie ahead, you need to stay in the air as much as possible—touch down to make contact with another company and then take off again.

Biz Dev gives you permission to run with ideas in a way that no traditional business growth channel could. **If you can imagine it, you can probably Biz Dev it.**

AvantGo, Inc., is a company that lets people get at familiar business applications through their wireless, Internet-enabled hand-held computers and Internet-enabled phones. AvantGo literally could not exist without Biz Dev. AvantGo works with various software firms to create modified interfaces for the desktop applications customers use at work, and the company partners with the *New York Times,* Amazon.com, MapQuest, TheStreet.com, Trip.com, and the Weather Channel to deliver their information and services through its channels to users.

Everyone wins. Users get the information they need in a unique blend of proprietary data, products, and travel info that every road warrior needs. E-commerce providers know that people will order on the run. Content providers extend their brand and their reach as people access their information (and related advertising) at the exact moment when they need it; talk about point of relevance delivery!

You've seen MapQuest all over the Internet. Hotels, businesses, tourist attractions, the baby sitter's house; if you want to get there in the real world, MapQuest is your virtual tour guide. How did MapQuest beat mapmaking giant Rand McNally at its own game? By tapping into the mapping data of a variety of technological partners and tying that together with marketing and distribution partners to provide a completely new service: directions on tap to wherever you want to go. They're now developing partners for the new wireless systems (like AvantGo)—including real-time traffic data. None of it would be possible without well-executed Biz Dev.

A Little Test

Most people want to think that they're bold risk takers.

So here's a little test to see where you fall on the Biz Dev spectrum: when someone approaches you in a meeting, or calls you, with a new idea that involves collaborating on targeting a single market segment, what is your first instinct—to clear your calendar of the mundane so you can jump on this opportunity? Or do you ask the person to put it in writing and you'll take a look at the proposal? If you clear your calendar, you get it. If you want to see a paper proposal (in triplicate!), you don't.

Partnership redefined

It used to be that if companies had partners, they had a few exquisitely selected companies that were nearly a match in terms of size and depth of resources. Squadrons of marketers, then lawyers, would hammer out complicated nondisclosure, trademark, protection of intellectual property, and non-compete agreements just so the partnership could become official. This process could take months. And what they had at the end was an agreement to share information on sensitive product development functions, perhaps, or to market to each other's customers in a clearly delineated way, surrounded by no-customer-poaching agreements.

The Biz Dev definition of partnership is quite different. In Biz Dev, partnership means that two companies have agreed **to share complementary technology, marketing resources and other inside information for the rapid deployment of a specific plan.** That plan might be to create a market, or reach a market in a new way.

The Biz Dev partnership has a short attention span. It may endure through many, varied projects aimed at that original market. Or the partnership may exist for a single project, and fade away as that target market changes and grows beyond the scope of the joint effort. The partnership may not work at all—you may both realize that your perceptions of the market are so different that you can't really work in tandem after all. And that's OK. You may be better matched for reaching a different market, at a different time, with a different approach.

These partnerships are not defined by legalities. They are sketched out in terms of the goals, not in terms of the protective language that seeks to insulate each partner from the other's foibles and potential missteps. Most business development executives formalize their partnerships with letters of intent, working agreements, or similar short statements. The point is to spell out the expectations and mutual goals of the two parties so that they can immediately move forward to capture the present market opportunity.

Redefining an alliance

Traditionally, an alliance is comprised of organizations that are all on the same side of an issue or controversy. That's what trade alliances are all about—the participants agree to put aside their competitive stances and focus on what they have in common, whether that's getting a piece of industry-favorable legislation through Congress or setting mutually beneficial technical standards. Industry alliances paved the way for fax protocols, allowing all fax machines to 'talk' to each other, for instance. The Internet itself is utterly dependent on commonly held technological standards agreed and acted upon by software and hardware companies allied with each other to develop and adhere to those standards. That's how my e-mail, sent through AOL, can show up intelligibly on your screen, which is supported by a Netscape browser.

Biz Dev is forcing the concept of the alliance down into more mundane operating agreements. Auction sites, industry trading sites, and similar venues assume that the businesses participating are allied for that function—they all agree, say, to pool their buying power to make joint bids on certain materials. Even more specifically, some alliances are formed to lock up exclusive agreements among companies that realize that their perspective and approach to a certain market is so similar that they may as well co-operate. There are even alliances at the individual level, as is the case with the shopping site Mercata.com, where people form "buying alliances" to drive prices down when buying as a group.

As with partnerships, alliances are fluid. Nothing is set in stone. If it works, do more with that ally. If it doesn't, formally end the alliance, or simply ignore it until it shrivels up and dies of neglect.

Biz Dev Buzz: Clone the alliances that work. Kill those that don't.

The three types of relationships

Generally, relationships focus on technology, channels, or marketing.

Technology Partners

Technological partnerships are typically the first that a new company creates. A start-up has to get the software it needs to support its vision. Because this vision is new to the market, chances are good that the software doesn't already exist in a tidy package. Hiring and directing a team of programmers takes too long, and is too inefficient (even if you could find them). The more effective, faster, smarter way to create the technology is to find one, two or three technology partners who offer significant components of the software and hardware that you need. Some companies may only work with one software vendor to develop a custom program that does the job. Others have to collaborate with a couple of vendors and one or several specialized hardware manufacturers. In mid-2000, for instance, companies breaking new ground in wireless Internet, delivering unique content over cell phones and personal digital assistants, needed a convergence of programming and the cooperation of the makers of phones and PDAs, so that those devices could accommodate the transmission and display of the content.

Clearly, a company that is using the consulting and engineering expertise of its technology partners, as well as licensing existing software, will pay for that privilege. But because the collaboration is intended to be ongoing, with all players consistently engaged in extending and refining the technology, the relationship goes far beyond the project mentality of a typical customer-vendor relationship. It is an ongoing partnership, and the credibility of the technology partners signals to the outside world that their service or product is going to be supported by some of the top brains in the industry.

Channel Partners

Even as the technology partnerships are put in place, channel partnerships are in the works. In the business-to-consumer world over the Internet, the mother of all channels is America Online. In the late 1990s, companies signed contracts committing them to tens of millions of dollars annually for what amounts to a slotting fee—the right to be a preferred retailer to AOL's 23-million-plus customers.

Channel partnerships may involve elements of advertising, such as co-sponsoring print ads, or guaranteeing a number of banner ads (usually triggered by a customer's profile as developed by an online direct marketing agency such as DoubleClick).

In the B2B space, channel partnerships are just as likely to be private-label as co-branded. Some B2B services, like a prefab package that enables small businesses to build their own Web sites, are provided for a fee and other considerations, to a site that offers the service under its own brand name. Other partnerships are co-branded, with both companies' participation visible to the user. Content providers, for instance, usually want to make sure that viewers know which service is providing the news feed or archive of product descriptions. A company that licenses its project management software to other sites wants users to know exactly who they are, in case the users decide to license the software for their own companies' internal use.

Channel partnerships usually involve payment to both companies involved, in the form of revenue sharing. The maker of the project management software gets an initial fee for licensing it to a business services site, but the services site tracks the number of customers that actually use the project management piece and the site then gets a cut of those fees.

Marketing Alliances

Marketing alliances are critical for blanketing your market with your company's logo and mission. In the Stone Age of the Internet, link exchanges were all we had in the way of marketing alliances. Now these alliances are much more complex, fluid, short-term, and market-sensitive than technology and channel partnerships. Marketing alliances mix a bit of what one company does with a bit of what another company does to deliver just the service or product that a customer segment needs at that point in time. You might collaborate with another company to create a unique product that you both market, but more often alliances are leveraged to create fresh market approaches with parts of products and services that both partners already have on hand. That way you can very quickly package and introduce a new product or service, gaining awareness and customers, without spending months developing wholly new products from the ground up.

Case Study: E*Trade, Schwab, and Merrill Lynch

Way back in 1994, many business leaders were dismissing the Internet as a flash in the tech pan—a glorified phone line. In 1996, when Amazon.com was just six months old, entrepreneurs started to catch the vision that they could sell directly through the Internet to anyone who had a computer and a modem. While eToys, Priceline, and Ebay were racing to be first in their categories (even as they were creating their categories), many executives in traditional, established businesses figured that all they needed to have was an online "presence."

Meanwhile, alternative channels for conducting business were quickly ramping up. Vertical trading portals, auction sites, and reverse auction sites were grabbing the attention of analysts and companies that weren't afraid to wade into the new technology. Still, many big companies brushed aside the potential that the Internet held for handling their tried-and-true sales, marketing, pricing, customer communication, and fulfillment procedures. As late as August 1998, Launny Steffens, an executive vice president with Merrill Lynch, dissed the entire new economy by declaring that, "The do-it-yourself model of investing, centered on Internet trading, should be regarded as a serious threat to Americans' financial lives."

Less than a year later, he took it back. With Charles Schwab's vaunted online trading services grabbing more market share every day, not to mention the daily defections of droves of consumers to E*Trade, DLJ Direct, Charles Schwab online and others, Merrill Lynch belatedly announced on June 1, 1999, that it was going to enable its clients to trade online—by the end of the year.

When Merrill Lynch, and hundreds of other traditional companies, finally **woke up** to what was happening all around them in plain sight, they realized that competitors had literally emerged out of nowhere. It used to be that Merrill Lynch and T. Rowe Price and other stock brokerages had the business all to themselves. When Charles Schwab launched his discount brokerage, all his competitors knew about it. They watched Schwab laboriously build his company, customer by customer, office by office.

Merrill Lynch was **blindsided** by the dramatic growth of Schwab's online operation as well as the runaway popularity of the upstart online brokerage houses in general. Steffens had plenty of company. The same "blindsided by the Net" scenario played out in industry after industry. Companies accustomed to tracking their competition's moves and growth were ambushed by the immediate success of online competitors. When Charles Schwab was making waves with the then-novel idea of a discount brokerage, he did it in plain sight. All the established brokerages could see him build his company step by step. They saw his advertising. They knew when he opened his first offices in each city, and as he gradually deepened and broadened his services. Their networks of market intelligence kept them informed.

And, though Schwab grew quickly, it also grew **organically**: the company followed a traditional growth path, even if its product was untraditional. Competitors could reasonably forecast how big Schwab might be in the coming year, and how it was gradually changing the investment landscape and investors' expectations. Competitors had plenty of time to formulate and test counter-arguments against the idea of using a discount broker. They had plenty of time to plan tactical moves and move their big advertising and marketing guns into place.

But the purely online brokers didn't follow this growth script. They didn't even acknowledge that there was a script to follow. Instead, they were born full-grown—offering from the beginning many, certainly the most popular, resources and services that the established brokerages offered.

The traditional industry was utterly taken by surprise. Where had these upstarts come from? How could they offer research reports, and portfolio management tools, and news reporting services all from the get-go? Why didn't they look like conventional start-ups, which appeared on the landscape and were easily monitored as they got going?

Here's why: these upstarts didn't grow step-by-step, as Schwab did. In fact, those menacing competitors weren't even very big. They leveraged reputations borrowed from their suppliers and used smoke and mirrors to look big fast, and in looking big, they scared the bejeebees out of their entrenched competition. They came off like the swaggering new kids on the block because they had the latest technology, the ability to respond immediately to their customers' growing expectations, and the technological kahunas to, seemingly, pull rabbits out of hats.

They didn't grab market share fast because they actually were big. They got it because they *acted* big. And they acted big because Biz Dev meant they weren't alone. They surrounded themselves with affiliations and partnerships. They didn't foray out there with just the expertise that they could squeeze out of their own tech teams: they leveraged the expertise of technology companies that already had experience creating and managing databases, building various elements of transactional Web sites, and linking new electronic modes of communication with already-existing trading and internal corporate electronic communications channels.

E*Trade didn't pretend that it had conference rooms full of wizened analysts. It partnered with Omega Research, Inc., an investment analysis software manufacturer, so that it could jointly sponsor seminars on investing.

E*Trade partnered with E-Loan, Inc., to offer home mortgages.

E*Trade didn't try to build a new home-distribution system; it partnered with WebTV Networks, Inc., to serve up investment services to American couch potatoes through their family room television sets. And all that happened in just the first quarter of 1998. No wonder Merrill Lynch did a 180 degree turn.

Touch-and-go Biz Dev can work for any company, whether it's a start-up, a first-generation new economy company, or a 150-year-old company started when the Industrial Revolution was the next best thing. **It's about where you're going, not where you've come from.**

Sure, it's easier for companies populated mainly by people who don't have long personal histories developing business the old way. And it's definitely easier to start a company with this model of business development woven in from the beginning than to convert platoons of old-economy executives to the new method.

But it can be done. It **is** being done.

Just ask the people at E*Trade and Charles Schwab online these days what they think of Merrill Lynch.

For the ten months after Steffens dismissed the value of the Internet for Lynch's customers, the company officially ignored the Internet. Let others jump into bed with dot-com trading sites. Let Charles Schwab continually improve its online trading functions, to the point where, in mid-2000, 80 percent of its trades were occurring online. Merrill Lynch did not care. At least, officially, it did not care.

Apparently, agitation for change was brewing just below the surface. On June 1, 1999, Merrill Lynch shocked Wall St. by announcing that it was going to enable its clients to trade over the Internet after all. Suddenly, all kinds of Internet-related announcements started popping out of Merrill Lynch. In August 1999, Merrill Lynch announced that it was using Vignette Corp.'s software as the platform for its Internet sites—a tacit admission that the investment firm needed to bring in outside technology providers to roll out the kind of quality online service that its clients expected of it. In December 1999, Merrill Lynch paired up with Multex.com to deliver investment information online to Merrill Lynch's own institutional clients. And, the online trading system for individual investors went live in December 1999.

Once Merrill Lynch got the hang of Biz Dev, **it couldn't stop**. In mid-March 2000, Merrill Lynch and five other venerable Wall St. brokerages announced that they were pooling their resources to form "Securities.Hub," an online trading venue for institutional investors around the world.

The brokerage business is a classic case where an upstart (E*Trade) partnered with everyone in sight to "be everywhere," and eventually they were everywhere. Their story shows how small companies can use Biz Dev to compete with, and beat, big companies. It shows how allies create momentum, and how that momentum can beat a huge bricks-and-mortar infrastructure. In short, it shows why Biz Dev works.

Recreate the playing field

Like the execs at Merrill Lynch, many corporate bigwigs are realizing that they must be quick and targeted in pursuing e-commerce openings. They know their industries intimately—where all the pockets of inefficiency are, the friction points that ruin people's days, the 'wouldn't-it-be-nice-if's." Many have watched in frustration as Internet upstarts have emerged from nowhere with claims of owning the market—just because they got there first.

Some big companies will see value in partnering with those upstarts, effectively putting a cash value on the first-mover advantage. In fact, in many cases it's more efficient and faster to buy or ally with a dot-com than for a huge company to attempt to push its e-commerce agenda to the top of its company's IT project list.

Other big-company executives will decide that they would rather create their own first-mover advantage by recreating the playing field. Instead of getting in on the buying forums and vertical marketplaces and alliances created by the upstarts, they are banding together to create their own buying forums and vertical marketplaces and alliances, ignoring the upstarts altogether.

In effect, they're putting a premium on **resources** over **speed**—even as they vow to build their own alliances rapidly. Of course, they're able to make that vow largely because of the technologies that many dot-com upstarts created to support their own alliances. Established companies have clearly bought into the alliance model and will be combining their own technological strengths.

Big companies are realigning their resources. What's not clear is whether they're yet fully grasping what's at stake: that they must deliver on the promise of their alliances to create new, value-added services and products. In April 2000, PricewaterhouseCoopers released its annual e-business survey measuring the success that big companies are having as they try to migrate functions to the Internet. Almost half of them reported that they have full-time units dedicated to e-business strategy. But more than half have no idea how to measure the success of their Internet business efforts. Almost half didn't even have any specific goals. (Maybe that's what all the people in those full-time units are busy doing: coming up with matrices and goals and measurement tools.)

Also in April 2000, the Gartner Group predicted that the long-term driver of business to business e-commerce wasn't going to be freestanding dot-coms, but rather hybrid models that combine the traditional strengths of existing companies, particularly in operations and distribution, with dot-com speed and focus.

Bigger companies, bigger expectations

Precisely because they *are* big established companies, expectations are higher for their alliances and their new ways of conducting commerce than they were for dot-com start-ups. Customers understandably were skeptical about whether or not newly unveiled online trading forums would work, and just as understandably are breathing a sigh of relief now that the big guys have taken the idea for their own. Customers expect the big companies to do it right. And to do it right, big companies must realign more than their trading interfaces. They must realize that many of the annoying dot-com start-ups have got valuable market experience and technological expertise that can be tapped to deepen those new electronic trading venues. Big companies that adopt Biz Dev as one of their bedrock marketing and technological development strategies are the ones that will succeed in e-commerce.

The great strength of Biz Dev is not that it levels the playing field. It doesn't.

What it does is **recreate** the playing field so that each player is positioned to play to his strength. What good is a level playing field, anyway? Every company has a premiere strength that can be leveraged by a partner to mutually create new markets, sales, and customer loyalty. It doesn't do anybody any good to level all that into a flat plane. We're not playing baseball, where a hit ball might end up anywhere on the field. Sure, when you're running to catch a ball, you want a level field.

But isn't it better to play the game of business like volleyball? The players are positioned closer to the net or further away, depending on their strengths. When the ball comes over the net, one team member passes it to another, and that one to another, until it's passed to the person in the best position, with the most power and strength, to spike it back over the net.

Biz Dev Buzz: Leverage your contacts to find out how your competitors are using Biz Dev—even before they make their announcements.

Check it out

We've found several sources of information invaluable for keeping track of who's allying with whom, and what the results are.

For a great site for reviewing and monitoring companies, take a look at **http://www.companysleuth.com**

For daily news about current computing or Internet issues, visit Eweek at **http://www.eweek.com**

If you want a full-featured site with constantly updated information for everyone on your team, from marketing folks to the tech staff, see **http://www.Internet.com**

For traffic numbers and other information on other sites, whether competitors or potential partners, see **http://www.alexa.com**

For information on markets and industries, some of which is free, visit **http://www.zapdata.com**

For hundreds of links to business information, some great, some not, see **http://www.brint.com**

Fuld is one of the premier competitive intelligence organizations, so this list is a handy compilation of the best sites for "snooping." Visit Fuld at **http://www.fuld.com/i3/index.html**

If you want a handy "mind-it" service that tells you when a competitor's site has changed, visit **http://www.netmind.com**

To search public records to uncover things like bankruptcies, real estate records, aircraft ownership, lawsuits, liens and a host of other data, use this inexpensive site: **http://www.knowx.com**

For a free counter and analysis tool that shows the last thirty hits by IP address, try The Counter. Useful for monitoring Web traffic—and checking to see if a competitor has visited. See **http://www.thecounter.com**. For a similar tool that is even more robust and full-featured, try WebTrends at **http://www.webtrends.com**

Here's a great place for demographics, stats and info about the Internet. **http://www.iw.com/daily/stats/index.html**

For weekly stats on Internet usage, including some Nielsen data, try **http://www.cyberatlas.com**

Periodicals

Of course, the following have fine Web sites too, but the print version is handier to take with you on the train, airplane or helicopter (although the Web sites are easier to search for specific information.)

Business 2.0—Well-designed business magazine deals with new economy issues with an emphasis on practicalities.

Fast Company—Ahead of the curve, fun, and full of good ideas about the E-conomy.

Industry Standard—Weekly that tracks every emerging, cresting and falling trend in e-business. A must-read.

Red Herring—Focuses mainly on how to leverage technology to grow your business.

Wall St. Journal—Daily coverage of breaking news of companies, e-com and traditional. Regular in-depth coverage of e-commerce and business development topics, often in special columns and sections.

Take Biz Dev to the next level!
For other resources, ongoing conversation, and the BizDev3.0 newsletter, join us at **http://www.BizDev3.com**

Step 1: Get into the Biz Dev mindset

As soon as the Starbelly business plan was finished, I looked at it on my computer screen and I thought, "How are we going to make this happen? It has 100 main points!"

I didn't have any kind of epiphany or revelation about Biz Dev.

We just had to get the job done. The team we assembled had to move fast to create value, and we couldn't create it all ourselves. We needed help—lots of it.

We were like travelers staring at the Sahara Desert—a whole lot of sand, and not much water. It would be impossible to walk straight across, even with camels. But if we could make friends with the nomads who own the oases, we would be able to network our way across the desert, from one oasis to the next.

We started to assemble our technology team, and I saw how the personal relationships of our early investors were bringing us into contact with immensely valuable investors and potential partners. We began to develop a Biz Dev mindset.

As we got better at managing all these new relationships, we began to look at the world differently, and we built our new business, one partner at a time.

We didn't get religion, or take a course—we just evolved a new way of thinking about business possibilities. We got the Biz Dev mindset.

In this chapter:

You've got to go with your hunch

Your job? Vision-spreader

Relationships are the currency

Put on your running shoes!

Are your partners celebrities?

Where is the Biz Dev training camp?

Look for give and take

Be a Biz Dev scout

Build, buy, or Biz Dev a team

Biz Dev Toolkit

You've got to go with your hunch

I'm not psychic, but I see that Biz Dev folks have an almost eerie ability to sense what services and products people and businesses are beginning to crave, even before they themselves have identified that craving.

In Biz Dev, I would say that **intuition** is the ability to seek out the partners who can deliver those products or services, timing your announcement so that the target audience says, "You read my mind!"

Biz Dev hunches come from:

"Business more than any other occupation is a continual dealing with the future; it is a continual calculation, an instinctive exercise in foresight."—
Henry R. Luce

- Imagining how something can be created **from nothing**.
- Constantly looking for the place where your own company's strengths could intersect with another company's strengths, to create more value for your **mutual customers**.
- Asking, "What if?" and "Why not?" when free-associating through news-papers, magazines, news wires, and PR announcements.
- Scanning **1.0 technology** not because it's cool all by itself, but to figure out how it could make life easier for your customers.
- Wondering **who is signaling** (maybe through other newly announced alli-ances) that they are interested in serving your clients?
- Asking yourself, "What are the particular **frustrations** that drive my customers nuts? What are the problems that I could solve for them, if I had some

partners? What everyday annoyances make my customers go home at night and kick the dog?"

Biz Dev experts internalize these ways of thinking so intensely that they spot possibilities where nobody else does. You can't pin this thought process down in an algorithm, you can't quantify it. Just get the flash! The Biz Dev mindset takes the flash and makes it a reality.

Case Study: The Trip

I was going to meet a guy flying into Chicago from New Mexico. He called to say his flight was being rerouted around a storm front over the Midwest. Then he called again—the plane was going up to Canada, to beat the thunderheads. I began wondering where he was, and when he would get in.

What if I could track anyone's flight, to see where it is, right now? Acting on that idea, business-travel Web site TheTrip.com partnered with the Federal Aviation Administration to show visitors exactly where a plane was on its flight path, for any given commercial flight.

Users went nuts. They love this service. It's exactly what they need to know, in real time ("Is Mark going to get here in time for this afternoon's presentation?")

Plus, the graphics make the process a lot of fun ("Hey, look, right now Mark's over Lake Erie!").

Now thousands of customers have another reason to come back to TheTrip.com. Value for the customers, and stickiness for the site: not bad for a service that didn't exist until someone thought, "What if?"

Here's how you might approach a problem, in the Biz Dev mindset.

Solving this problem will not be just a matter of tweaking our customer service, or hinting at ways our customers can work around it.

This problem is an enjoyable little puzzle that can be deconstructed into parts, and each part has a solution.

We have one part of the solution. Other companies surely have other parts.

Flash! Together, we can solve this problem, make our customer happy, and make some money along the way.

Your job? Vision-spreader

How come Tony Robbins fills stadiums with 50,000 people? How can Colin Powell have an 86 percent approval rating? They show you what you can do to make your life better; they inspire people.

"A leader is a dealer in hope."
—Napoleon

Like a person, a business wants to get involved. A business wants to be swept off its feet, it wants to be part of a larger production, like a movie. Your business wants to be inspired.

A Biz Dev mindset can motivate the business, pulling the whole company along. That's why Biz Dev starts with pictures of what **might** be possible.

Intangible as they seem at first, those visions inspire your staff and your potential partners.

Inspiration is viral—spread it!

Inspiration is essential for acceptance. In Biz Dev, if you do not inspire, you cannot execute. That's not true in other parts of business. In collecting accounts receivable, for instance, you don't have to inspire anyone. But in Biz Dev you have to pull a lot of old thinkers along inside the company, and, outside, you have to inspire partners.

Odd, but your inspiration is part of what elicits trust in potential partners, particularly among start-ups. And that inspiration spreads.

As your company develops a track record and reputation for following through on whatever deals that the Biz Dev team has negotiated, your partners' trust is validated.

Now it's easier to inspire additional partners with visions of how your companies can work together because there is **proof** that your inspiration translates into reality.

Inspiration gets your other employees on board, too.

Heck, they might reasonably assume that all the Biz Dev staff does is travel, talk on the phone and do deals. Especially in traditional companies that have climbed to the top of their heap through linear, predictable growth, employees don't have any yardsticks for measuring the success of Biz Dev.

When you inspire them with your vision, you pull them into the process. They begin to contribute their own ideas, and work together better with each other, and with your partners. Inspiration is an upward cycle.

"Create a cause, not a business."

—Gary Hamel, *Fortune*

A reporter once asked the British novelist Kingsley Amis about inspiration. Amis said, "I only write when I am inspired, so I arrange to be inspired every morning at 9 AM."

Biz Dev Buzz: Part of getting into the Biz Dev mindset is arranging to be inspired on a regular basis.

Stories, not products, matter most

"We are in the twilight of a society based on data. As information and intelligence become the domain of computers, society will place more value on the one human ability that cannot be automated: emotion.

"Imagination, myth, ritual—the language of emotion—will affect everything from our purchasing decisions to how we work with others.... Companies will need to understand that their products are less important than their stories."

—Rolf Jensen, Copenhagen Institute for Future Studies

Relationships are the currency

When I want a ticket to a big concert, I know I can go camp out all night in line, or pay a fortune to a broker—or call my friends, to see who has an extra ticket. That way, I save time, and have more fun at the event, because I'm hanging out with a buddy.

Going through relationships can mean avoiding hassles—and enjoying yourself. That's the role of Biz Dev.

And that's why I think relationships are the currency of business, today.

We're no longer in an economy of objects, but an economy of relationships.

I was in Detroit last week, visiting the place I grew up, and I drove past the General Motors plant. I spent two minutes on the highway (going sixty miles per hour) just driving past one plant, and it was still going—that plant must be two miles long. I realized that the Internet Capital Group recently had a market cap of almost a third of GM, but you could drive past the entire ICG building in few seconds. Assembling atoms is just a lot less important than it used to be. Nowadays, the value is in putting companies and people together.

Biz Dev is about connecting pieces, not making them.

We used to manage assets but now we manage connections.

In the old days, we knew other folks, we networked, we built up our Rolodexes. Now the entire business has to network, and make new connections. The business is like a person. We used to say, "It's who you know," but now it's what other businesses the business knows.

As businesses become wired together, the friction, frustration and cost of mutual coordination declines.

Friction is delay, drag, sparks coming out of the brake pads. Biz Dev is anti-friction.

In the old days if an order didn't arrive, you had to call the company, ask for the tracking number, call UPS or FedEx and wait for a clerk to look it up. Now you double-click the tracking number in your e-mail or account, and get taken right to the delivery service, to find out where your package is. Because of that strategic alliance, you save ten or fifteen minutes, and a lot of friction for both companies, and consumers.

As you reduce those frictions, you are freed to concentrate wholly on what you do best.

At Starbelly, we came to the conclusion that because of the Internet, the value of time has increased exponentially. Yes, back in the industrial revolution, the assembly line speeded up the whole manufacturing process, and minted money.

With the invention of fast food, customers could save a half hour—and McDonald's franchisees made fortunes. But the Internet says, "If you can save someone three minutes, you have created millions (perhaps billions) in value, because those three minutes multiplied by an infinite number of transactions in an industry will actually produce years of time savings." The whole B2B world says, "The time you save by not looking at a hundred catalogs could be worth millions." The value in seconds is even greater on the Internet than

Time is money, now more than ever! If you save time, you create exponential value.

at the drive-through, so **using the Web to eliminate friction builds value fast.**

You need to know how to run your business, but you don't have to own every single little operation and support function. You can reach out to everyone you know to find other companies that can do for yours what they do best.

That approach frees your company to become even better at whatever it does best. And the relationships woven by Biz Dev are what hold all that together.

The business depends on the network of relationships, and, in a sense, the business becomes the relationships.

The Biz Dev staff orchestrates, synchronizes and coordinates the information, power and pace of developing those critical relationships—and therefore, potentially, drives the company's growth.

I'm addicted to the magazine *Business 2.0*, which covers the E-conomy. I kept noticing articles written by Mohanbir Sawhney, a professor at Northwestern University's Kellogg School of Management, here in Chicago. I was looking for fantastic business growth experts to be on the Starbelly board of advisors, so I checked out Sawhney's ideas on his Internet site.

I was astounded: everything that had been dawning on me was beautifully laid out. And Sawhney practices what he preaches right on his site. In order to get full access to his contact list, you have to agree to register, giving your own name and contact info.

That list is open to everyone who registers—in effect creating a loose community of people who have read Sawhney's views. He's managing these relationships, sure, but anyone who contributes to the list gets his Rolodex—an **instant network** of like-minded folks. Not bad for a little typing!

Put on your running shoes!

Reading Sawhney's Web site was like reading my own business diary. I was already gravitating towards a networked model of business growth. Here was a professor, essentially telling me that I was right and that I should go for it.

The best time to act on an idea is now. Right now.

Of course, I had to talk with him.

Starbelly's offices are on the north side of Chicago, a short drive from Northwestern.

I called Sawhney and got right through. I gave him my elevator pitch. He suggested that we get together in a couple of weeks.

"Well, I have time right now," I said. "Can we talk if I get to Northwestern in eight minutes?"

"Oh, sure," he said. I don't think he really expected me to show up.

I knew that if I didn't seize the moment, I'd lose a chance to show Sawhney that I was so serious about Biz Dev that I wasn't going to wait a civilized two weeks to talk to him and persuade him to be on our advisory board. I was looking for folks who moved fast.

I got in the car.

As I drove along Lake Michigan's shoreline to Northwestern, I realized that our immediate agreement to get together had already started to deliver results: I felt a sense of investment

In America, an hour is forty minutes.

—German saying

Speed is not sloppiness. It's getting the deal done **before** the customers realize they want the new product, or the extra service.

"While we ponder when to begin, it becomes too late to act."

—Quintilian

in the relationship, and I thought Sawhney would, too.

I walked into Sawhney's office and I said, "I know I just have ten minutes. We're revolutionizing an industry, and you have to hear about this." Of course, the ten minutes turned into half an hour. I told him, "We're going to transform an industry. You've got to be involved!" He said "Yes"—and he has been on our advisory board ever since.

Moving fast to set up a relationship—that's a big part of the Biz Dev mindset.

It's a **different rhythm**. You don't drive any faster, or work any more efficiently, but you don't accept conventional delays either.

Charles Ardai, CEO of Juno Online, says he spends 25 percent of his time on Biz Dev. His focus is speed to market.

"You start out with the premise that you don't have much time, so you build the core competency and partner for the rest."

His team of 300 built the e-mail service at their heart, outsourced customer service (700 technicians), partnered with an ad agency, and allied with lots of content partners for feeds of health info, movie reviews, news, sports items, travel tips, even weather. "Those partnerships allowed us to get started without huge capital expenditures."

Negotiate in real time

In the Biz Dev mindset, negotiating is like breathing. It's funny, but it makes me think of this time when I asked a karate master what to do about breathing, and he said, "Don't stop."

The ind2ind site focuses on industry-to-industry transactions.

With Biz Dev, D.J. Long has transformed ind2ind from a stodgy software company into a B2B machine. I asked him what it takes to get into the Biz Dev mindset. He's met hundreds of Biz Dev executives, and he knows which personal characteristics it takes to get in and stay in this particular game.

"This has to do with real-time negotiation. There are not long cycles here, and there is not a funnel of qualification of criteria in the traditional selling sense," he says.

"You have to think and act quickly and not be afraid to make mistakes. You have to focus on getting things done and executed rapidly. The person on the other side of the table is talking to your competitors."

When I talk with friends who work in big companies, I hear about the eleven-teenth committee meeting, the nine months' delay, the incredible drag on their spirits, the constant friction. I can't imagine an environment more contrary to the essence of what we all know to be our E-conomy.

Reminds me of those movies where the guy has a crush on a girl, but never asks her out to the prom. You keep asking, "When are you going to get it?"

Have you ever been at a flea market, and seen some item you really liked, but passed on by, and when you came back, found that it was sold? Remember those moments of frustration? Biz Dev is the opposite of frustration. "**Go for it**" is our motto.

Are your partners celebrities?

Biz Dev lets your company bask in shared glory.

Ever notice how when you go to a fancy restaurant, you somehow feel special, right away. Or when you dress up, and are around others who are well dressed, you feel good. Or when you meet a celebrity, you feel yourself becoming part of their aura. The Biz Dev mindset says "Surround yourself with celebrities—businesses that are reputable, and make you look good with your customers." You need these companies as partners, not vendors or outsourcers.

One lesson I learned in the development of Starbelly is that our partnerships would determine our success. Partners would allow us to develop our industry realignment immediately. And partners would help us get our message out. In fact, it turned out that our partners often became our best customers.

Before Starbelly, I was used to setting the terms for my suppliers and vendors. "Here's my best offer—take it or leave it."

In a lot of ways, suppliers had become commodities. It's a pain to go look for a new supplier, but there's so little to differentiate among makers of generic t-shirts and sweatshirts that loyalty was never the main issue. They didn't add much value to my company's process of applying silk-screened or embroidered logos to the shirts.

But I had to do a 180 when Starbelly was launched.

Suddenly I had no choice but to find reliable technology companies who so deeply understood the Starbelly model that they'd commit to a long-term, gut-wrenching, high-pressure project to create the e-commerce infrastructure we needed for our site (in six months, thanks). This was no take-it-or-leave-it proposition. I needed their expertise, but, just as important, I needed the credibility that I gained by citing them as our technology partners. **Reflected glory**, sure—but I'll take reflected glory over no glory any day.

As I met with our technology folks in our weekly business strategy brainstorming sessions, I began to realize: this is what business development is all about. These guys are an integral part of our success. I can't disengage them and plug in any old bunch of program-mers—not if I expect to get the same level of enthusiasm.

It wasn't just that our team got along great with theirs. We had coalesced into a single, unified team, with an ongoing commitment to make the business plan into a business.

Managing relationships, moving fast to establish new relationships, nurturing those relationships into genuine partnerships—those are key synapses in the Biz Dev mindset.

Where is the Biz Dev training camp?

To form the core of our Biz Dev team at Starbelly, we recruited the director of marketing at an insurance company, a public relations expert, a sales person used to making calls every day, an entrepreneur who had never worked inside a company before, and a couple of lawyers. What they all had in common was, they understood the approach: Let's talk to everyone, let's grow through affiliations and alliances.

Also, everyone was able to step out of his or her training. There are a dozen formal career tracks that could translate into Biz Dev, but the people who can make the leap are willing to let go of their backgrounds.

Make mistakes! Then make sure you learn from them.

Biz Dev hasn't been around for more than half a dozen years. So most Biz Dev folks have moved into this role from **sales** (where they often felt they were constrained from communicating the whole picture to their customers) or **marketing** (where tradition dictated that the company should have a Lone Ranger attitude, rarely collaborating with other companies). Some are **lawyers** (the ones with some business sense) and some used to be **consultants** (the ones who can manage follow-through for the deals they cut).

If you feel drawn to the Biz Dev mindset, chances are that you can leverage much of your prior business experience to create or win a Biz Dev position for yourself.

But Biz Dev is different from each of these traditional roles.

You have to have the soul of a diplomat, as well, and the dreams of an explorer or astronaut—not afraid to define a new territory, able to persuade others that the rewards will make it worth overcoming the dangers along the way, eager to open up that new land for others to enter.

That's why so many Biz Dev folks are pioneers. Trailblazing is part of the mindset.

Biz Dev folks are:

- **Visionary**—able to perceive "1 + 1 = 3" potential in the collaboration of her company with another company.
- **Fearless**—willing to weather rejection and hesitation on the part of others as he explains his vision to them.
- **Persuasive**—able to convince others, both inside her company and outside, of the rewards to be reaped if they work together to create the new service or product.
- **Determined**—able to nail down the specifics of the agreement and close the deal and then lead the effort within his company to deliver the components required by the deal.

- **Inclusive**—eager to draw others into the process, especially mentoring potential Biz Dev gurus within his company.

- **Technical**—able to grasp the essentials of the technology, production and logistics required to support her company's part of the collaboration.

- **Self-disciplined**—able to pursue achievable dreams, put pipe dreams on the back burner, and know the difference.

- **Team-builders**—so that others in her company will come to understand, respect and buy into the power of Biz Dev as a growth engine for their company and their careers.

And, by the way, you might as well add "Willing to make lots of mistakes" to this list. If your team is not making mistakes, they're not doing their job.

Biz Dev Buzz: Real Biz Dev aims to collaborate with the partner in a genuine give-and take, changing the way you both do business.

Look for give and take

The Biz Dev mindset is not just sales under a new business title. You are not looking for someone to buy something from or sell something to. You want to create value together, collaboratively. In Biz Dev you work together to create opportunities.

I've had people call me, introducing themselves as Biz Dev experts and then fishing around for ways they can use Starbelly as a distribution channel for their company's stuff.

They don't even hint that an affiliation with their company or a co-marketing deal could bring anything of value to our customers. They're sales people pretending to be Biz Dev.

If you're in sales, say so. Then I won't get you off the phone as fast as I hang up on these pretenders.

Andrew Gelman, who directs Biz Dev for an Internet media site, says the same thing. "I get three or more phone calls a day from people who say they want a strategic partnership when what they really want is for us to buy something," he says. "You have to understand your partners' needs and problems, and how to satisfy those to your own advantage, too."

Biz Dev BS Detector: If the transaction has an endpoint, you are talking to a sales guy, no matter what his business card says. If the deal leads to lots of new possibilities, you are dealing with a real Biz Dev person.

Litmus test: If there is a purchase order involved, you are in sales.

Sales	Biz Dev
• Finite time line	• Ongoing life
• PO involved	• Chance to collaborate
• Exchange of products	• Share product creation

Sales is **not** Biz Dev!

Be a Biz Dev scout

If Biz Dev is such a young discipline, it must be hard to find qualified, experienced Biz Dev honchos, right?

Yes and no.

Because Biz Dev starts as a mindset, successful Biz Dev experts can come from a variety of backgrounds—as long as they understand how Biz Dev differs from all the jobs they've held before.

My friend Ted Martin, who's an executive recruiter, tops in his field, says that marketers, consultants, business lawyers, and venture capitalists can usually transfer their skills to Biz Dev—with a little work.

- **Marketers** often need to acquire tougher negotiation skills, but at least they are used to living with the results of their deals, long-term.
- **Consultants** often are great at vision and passion, but short on negotiation and follow-through.
- **Lawyers** and **VCs** are amazing, awesome negotiators, but they usually collect their fees on the way out the door. The challenge for them is to learn patience, to live with and continue to evolve the partnerships and alliances they fought hard to reel in.

Regardless of his or her immediate background, Martin says that the single most valuable asset a Biz Dev executive brings is a **golden Rolodex**.

Martin asks Biz Dev job candidates to outline the best deals they've done and name the players—the stars can do that. Their best deals are the ones that are more than the sum of the relationships, in win-win partnerships.

Build, buy, or Biz Dev a team

There are three ways to pull together a great Biz Dev team—build, buy, or Biz Dev it.

Build

Develop internal candidates who already show an intuitive grasp of Biz Dev. They are the ones who are always popping up with new ways to go to market or suggesting that your company pair up with another one to come up with unique products or marketing channels. If your company is traditional, these folks have nowhere to go. Look for someone who's frustrated with the status quo, cramped by the routine—she'll surprise you.

Figure out where these folks congregate. What happens to their serendipitous observations? How can your company create a way to act on them?

If you already have some Biz Dev folks on board, have them mentor the newbies and circulate them throughout a variety of Biz Dev projects, doing due diligence on potential partners, or leading partnership care teams that cultivate and deepen relationships with existing partners.

Biz Dev Buzz: Biz Dev gurus can't help themselves—they practice Biz Dev in whatever jobs they currently have.

Buy

If you're going to go out and buy a Biz Dev person, get it right. Find a great Rolodex. Look for people who have already been trained in the Darwin School of Biz Dev, over the last

"Early adopters—those most likely to embrace Biz Dev, especially in traditional organizations—account for about 16% of an entire market.

"Innovative, but not cutting-edge companies see the benefits, jump on board, and become potential partners and allies. This early majority accounts for another 34% of a total market.

"Companies that say 'I'll believe it when I see that it works,' the late majority, comprise another 34%.

"Those companies that are dragged kicking and screaming into Biz Dev or any major change are the laggards and account for the remaining 16 %."

—*Network to Net Worth*, Credit Suisse First Boston Corporation

Mindset: a way of thinking, a view of the world, a cultural perspective.

few years. Don't settle for someone who has done the expected deals inside a closed industry. Look for someone who has done the unexpected deals, matching up competitors, for example, or two companies that had nothing to do with each other. Look for true wackiness. Behind the wacky funky deal is someone who really gets it.

Shamelessly recruit Biz Dev superstars that you encounter on the other side of the table. (Don't bother with any Starbelly Biz Dev VPs; they're perfectly happy, thanks.) Broaden your search a little by looking for the key Biz Dev characteristics in people in sales, marketing and consulting.

Martin says that you'll face stiff competition, as Biz Dev gurus are just as in demand as programmers and technical development specialists.

Biz Dev a team

Start-ups may be able to hook up with complementary firms to put together joint pitches to potential partners. Rely on the expertise of your bankers, lawyers, and marketing and technical consultants to create project teams aimed at reeling in particular partners.

Professionals, wake up! Your colleagues who leave town could be perfect partners.

Do that a few times, and you'll be growing fast enough to support your own crack internal team.

This doesn't work long-term, as you'll have to have Biz Dev staff purely devoted to your company's mission, but you will find many occasions when collaborating with another firm gives you the best chance of persuading a much larger company to be a partner.

Peter Black, a principal with Mancini Duffy,

an architectural firm, has found that architects who leave to start their own practices—either in different cities, or in other areas of expertise—can turn out to be perfect partners.

He will often team with them to create joint proposals for clients that are too big for either firm to pursue independently.

"The specialized expertise of the smaller firm complements Mancini Duffy's broader, more general experience."

Caution

D.J. Long of ind2ind, points out that you have to recognize that Biz Dev can be threatening to old-economy thinkers in their own companies.

They need to be reassured that they're coming along for the ride, too. Long has seen that deer-in-the-headlights look plenty of times on the faces of seasoned sales people: it's the look they flash when they feel a stab of fear that business development will boot them right into the unemployment line.

"Salespeople absolutely feel threatened. They fear being rendered useless," he says.

"Sometimes business development has to do its own Biz Dev in-house."

Biz Dev Toolkit: Director of Business Development Job Description

Responsible for strategic alliance development and management of third-party content, distribution, marketing and product companies collaborating with the employer. This includes identifying and developing new partnerships for new product and service development and ongoing rollout of products and services through existing partnerships. Internally, director will work closely with the product and content development groups, the technology teams responsible for linking with partners, and various marketing and corporate communications staffs.

Required experience includes setting up and negotiating business models and agreements.

> "I use not only all the brains I have, but all I can borrow."
>
> —Woodrow Wilson

Skills include leadership, project management, relationship management, and strong negotiation skills. Experience with product development a plus. Solid technology and quantitative skills. Excellent written, oral and presentation capabilities.

Other desired skills: content development manager, business development, licensing, portal, strategic alliances, Web, Internet, marketing. Position requires 25 percent travel.

Check it out

The site for the magazine *Business 2.0* is a fantastic resource for Biz Dev, and the whole E-conomy, at **http://www.business2.com**

ind2ind lets you auction stuff off, offer it for sale, or place a classified ad, industry to industry, at their site, **http://www.ind2ind.com**

If you have a fast connection, and like to watch super Flash, visit the Mancini Duffy site, and browse their philosophy: **http://www.manciniduffy.com**

To find out what Ted Martin, the number one recruiter for venture capitalists, is up to, go to his site, **http://www.martinptrs.com**

Sign up for the relationships, download great articles on the E-conomy from Mohanbir Sawhney's site, at **http://www.mohansawhney.com**

Find out where an airplane is right now, by playing with the Flight Tracker at **http://www.thetrip.com**

Take Biz Dev to the next level! For other resources, ongoing conversation, and the BizDev3.0 newsletter, join us at **http://www.BizDev3.com**

Step 2: Find allies everywhere

In Biz Dev I have only two unchanging alliances—to my company and to my customers. All other bets are off.

- I can't rule out any company, because it might become an ally.
- I can't separate the world into friend and foe, because yesterday's enemy may be today's best partner.
- I can't assume I own one territory, and my competition owns another, because, together, we may soon share an expanding turf.
- I can't even think I live in a particular industry, because the whole industry may dissolve within eighteen months.
- And I can't count on any alliance lasting very long, either. The old assumptions have gone poof.

Competition just isn't what it used to be. In a shifting landscape, I have to keep looking everywhere for allies. That means:

- Imagining what it would be like to ally myself with this company;
- Discovering allies in areas I never even thought of before;
- Punching through barriers that keep my company isolated.

In this chapter:

Get creative! There's nothing you can't Biz Dev!

Choose neutrality

Blow-the-door-open policy

Stay non-exclusive (most of the time)

Make a bigger pie with your competition

Let alliances redefine your business

Test the limits of openness

Get creative! There's nothing you can't Biz Dev!

A year ago, if I'd asked the owner of my neighborhood gas station whether CNN could be a strategic ally, he would have laughed in my face. Sure, the clerk always had Oprah on next to the security monitor, but that was about as TV as the place got.

I'd pull my Jeep up to the pump, scan my credit card, lift the nozzle, unscrew the cap, pump. My mind was dead. The only distraction was watching the little numbers total up the gallons and dollars. So I imagined how I would Biz Dev a gas station.

I asked myself, what if the boss took a bigger view? What would that mean to me, as a customer?

The old-style gas station

Anything can be Biz Dev'd. Anything!

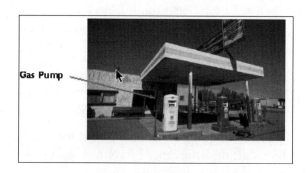

Gas Pump

Well, I'm already targeted. By definition, I'm a car owner, and I have some interest in keeping my Jeep going.

And the gas pump is already doing e-commerce, in a way, since it processes my credit card with one swipe.

What if they added a screen telling me about a sale at the Target store across the parking lot, or the lunch specials at the restaurant next door? What about ads for new cars—or recall notices? Heck, I've already told them who I am, by giving my credit card, so how about a little more partnering—a message like, "We partner with Jiffy Lube. And because you bought gas here, we're going to print out a coupon for half-off on a lube job. Is that OK with you?"

Presto! The gas pump has been transformed from a passive, dead piece of machinery into a kiosk telling me something I might really like to hear—courtesy of the friendly gas station owner, and his local business partners, who want me to think of them the next time the engine starts knocking.

Now this station **means more** to me. The inert objects become active, even interesting, and so I'm more likely to come here, even if I have to drive past other stations. And the owner is taking my minute of down time as I pump gas, and selling that minute to a bunch of partners who can use it better.

Biz Dev can make an object, and a company, mean more to the consumer. In-store coupons, satellite navigation in the car, wireless PDAs hooking up to nearby stores— these are just a few of the objects that Biz Dev has made smarter.

Next-generation gas station

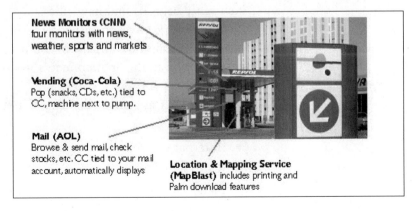

News Monitors (CNN)
four monitors with news, weather, sports and markets

Vending (Coca-Cola)
Pop (snacks, CDs, etc.) tied to CC, machine next to pump.

Mail (AOL)
Browse & send mail, check stocks, etc. CC tied to your mail account, automatically displays

Location & Mapping Service (MapBlast) includes printing and Palm download features

It was just a daydream. But I've seen it coming true in a gas station in Santa Fe, New Mexico, when CNN comes alive on a TV screen as soon as I swipe my credit card to buy gas. And now BP Amoco announces BP Connect, stations you can modem into as you drive, getting advance authorization for gas so you don't have to wait and swipe. At the pump you can get online maps, weather, and traffic. You can even order food prepared inside, to pick up when you finish fueling.

Biz Dev Buzz: Any deal that doesn't sell out my own company or my customers could, possibly, be a deal that could be made.

Choose neutrality

Neutrality has been rewarding for tough little countries like Switzerland. Selling to both sides of two world wars, staying out of trouble, making money—the Swiss have made a good business out of neutrality. You can too.

We're brought up to think of neutrality as cowardly, wishy-washy, fuzzy. But in Biz Dev, neutrality helps us avoid getting caught up in old wars.

Why choose sides? Be ready for anything.

Neutrality helps us find **new allies**.

Neutrality is positive, an **active decision**.

Neutrality means no company or competitor is off limits, taboo, or inconceivable as a partner.

Taking a neutral stance, Biz Dev is not hemmed in by:

- Internal turf wars
- Corporate feuds
- What the market is used to

- Barriers sanctified by tradition
- Differences in corporate culture
- Long-held prejudices about other companies

In all these battles, you win by being neutral.

Outgrowing the if-onlies

When I see myself saying, "If only…," I realize I am letting myself settle for some kind of constraint.

In meetings, conferences, negotiations, I hear "If only" all the time, followed by "But, but, but."

- **If only** we had the technology to make our services easily accessible to that market segment…but…we can't afford to divert resources from our core operations.

- **If only** we could get some internal expertise in this area that complements our other services, we'd save our customer time and hassles and make a little more money for delivering the convenience…but…we can't afford to re-create that particular wheel.

- **If only** we could talk with the audience of that big portal, specialized content site, or travelers or mothers or customers of distributors of construction equipment…but…we're stuck with the usual channels of trade magazines and traditional advertising and marketing.

Traditionally, people thought, "If only." Biz Dev thinks, "**What an opportunity!**"

Through Biz Dev, the 'if-onlies' are within your reach. The other companies that have the technology, operational skills and ear of their markets are potential partners.

Sure, they want certain things from you—maybe money, maybe reciprocal access to your markets, maybe a specialized version of your service—but negotiating a good agreement is part of what Biz Dev is all about. You win, your partners win, and most of all, your customers win.

Neutrality means the freedom to consider every alliance

You are free to interpret your company's vision and direction in any way the market dictates—today.

The competitor you fear might become the partner you love.

In net markets like those in chemicals, auto parts, agricultural equipment and supplies, we see companies in well-established categories putting aside some differences to recognize that they gain more by owning a piece of the joint action than they do by staying out of it.

To the buyers, the net marketplace says, "Every player in this group is willing to sacrifice a bit to give you product descriptions, good prices, and all-in-one-place ordering. We give you convenience and volume." Often the resulting service is better than what a customer would get going from one company to another, getting bids, comparing them, haggling individually.

"I have learned to use the word *impossible* with the greatest caution."
—Werner von Braun

Only the companies that choose neutrality can get the benefits. When American Airlines,

Delta, United, and others ally to offer an airline supersite, they create a much larger critical mass than any of them could put together individually. The site has more **gravity**, and pulls more people.

Case Study: Covisint

Ford set up a B2B exchange with its suppliers, the Ford Auto Xchange, and General Motors set up the TradeXchange, only to discover that they could save even more money combining with Daimler Chrysler and Renault/Nissan to make a single gigantic exchange, Covisint. Over the course of a week, representatives from the car makers drew a diagram on a white board, showing how the exchange would work, and **signed the white board—that was the binding document.**

Adam Gutstein and John Sviokla of Diamond Technology Partners, who helped put together Covisint, the B2B exchange for the auto industry, say that the first rule for building an exchange is to think big. "If you can't deliver a huge volume of transactions to the exchange, it will likely never develop critical mass. You might as well not bother."

You have to figure out what you compete on, too. The Big Three automakers buy parts worth $250 billion every year, but before creating the exchange, they had to decide that they did not compete on purchasing. "They decided they compete on car design, innovation in engines, and on-board technology. Moreover, for GM and Ford, roughly half of their profits come from their financing divisions."

Think of the way companies put aside their differences to form trade associations, lobby for tax breaks and tariffs, carry out market research, or set standards.

The members suspend hostilities long enough to get work done that benefits everyone in the association.

For those purposes, the members are willing to cooperate even though they're still jockeying for power, shoving back and forth in closed-door meetings, beating each other to market, fighting over customers outside.

For a particular benefit, though, they are willing to show **selective neutrality.**

Reducing the cost of purchasing, then, made sense for all. "The National Association of Purchasing Managers says it currently costs an average of $79 for a corporation to handle a purchase order. CommerceOne, a start-up that does online purchasing for companies, says that cost falls to $6 when the process is automated over the Internet."

Also, by exposing the manufacturers' current inventory levels, customer demand, special alerts, and supplier capacities, the auto makers reduce their need for stockpiling, forecasting supplies more accurately, and scheduling their manufacturing more reliably. As Fed Chair Alan Greenspan said recently, **"Information is a substitute for inventory."**

Of course, to avoid antitrust busters, the exchange has to remain open to all comers, protect proprietary and competitive information, and allow participants to shop elsewhere if they wish.

Case Study: Solutia

One day in February 2000, four guys knocked on Chip Merritt's door. Merritt, Director of E-Business for Solutia, Inc., a chemical manufacturer, was spending most of his time wrestling with customers' proprietary electronic data interface (EDI) systems—an expensive and tedious chore.

The four guys were from Ethyl Corp., a competitor, and they had a better idea. They wanted to know if Solutia would participate in an Internet-based hub, along with twenty other chemical manufacturers, to support a common, Internet-based market platform. Such a hub

"Do not fall into the delusion that your advancement can be accomplished by crushing others."
—*Cicero*

would mean no more separate EDI links to individual suppliers and customers, no more months programming each link, and access to new customers, along with the risk of seeing some existing customers take a good look at competitors.

Usually, it takes Merritt weeks to herd ideas through Solutia's executive ranks. It took him four days to get an executive stamp of approval, and a $4 million commitment to the Envera Network.

For both customers and manufacturers, the benefits are obvious—they can issue purchase orders, invoices, shipping notices, and payments through the exchange. They can track shipments so manufacturing customers will know exactly when supplies will arrive. No more calling the customer service rep, who calls the trucking company, who calls the trucker on a cell phone, who reports that he's ten miles east of Peoria, and tracing that information back through the chain so the customer finds out tomorrow where his shipment was—on the road—yesterday.

If the four guys from Ethyl had knocked on Solutia's door a few years ago, Merritt says that Solutia wouldn't have opened the door. It just wasn't interested in co-operating with other companies—especially not competitors.

"Now we are putting people in position to do just that," he says. "Companies are looking for **connections in every direction**. We all know that there are going to be some great opportunities and we're all wrestling with lists of ideas. This is a beautiful time to be approaching companies with new ideas."

When you are open, you are free to pounce on rapidly emerging opportunities.

Biz Dev Buzz: Because I never know where my next, best alliance will come from, I cannot afford to arbitrarily erase any company—or group—from my radar screen.

Blow-the-door-open policy

For my parents, growing up during the cold war, Russia was frightening, and communism was a serious threat. But for my friends and me, the cold war just wasn't a factor. Perhaps that's why we're willing to talk to competitors. There is no iron curtain for us.

As our team got Starbelly rolling, we began to see that because we were doing something new, that involved so many suppliers, we were really setting standards for the industry. So we invited the industry in, to see what we were up to.

We invited every competitor, every supplier, every customer, to come in and look at our business plan.

We figured, heck, we think we have a better team, we're quicker, we know what we're doing—let's tell them exactly what we are doing, because we cannot get where we want to go without them becoming a part of the operation.

We showed **everyone** around, told them just what we were doing. Some just shook hands and left as fast as they could. Others joined up on the spot. We developed unique relationships with lots of parties. And we got together with the biggest company in the business, HALO, so now, together, we can redefine the industry.

That wouldn't have happened if we had kept our doors—and minds—locked shut.

No one needs non-disclosure agreements any more, because the idea is no longer a competitive advantage. The idea is a commodity. Execution is what adds real value.

Biz Dev open-mindedness is:

- Understanding your company's **strengths** well enough to not be threatened by other companies that compete with you directly or indirectly;

- Understanding your **markets** well enough to know what your customers want, and how badly they want it, so you can measure the value of ceding some market share;

- Treating competitors with **respect** and cordiality so you can cooperate;

- Realizing that market forces may converge in such a way that your customers are best served if you cooperate **across traditional battle lines.**

Don't misunderstand: **you are not losing your competitive edge or going soft when you force yourself to give serious consideration to every possibility.** It's unlikely that Stamps.com (profiled in this chapter for its astounding ability to partner in many directions) will ever get in bed with E-stamp.com. They are head-to-head competitors with a mutual death wish. In the old world, though, both companies would focus enormous amounts of energy trying to lock up chunks of market exclusivity, drawing all their partners onto one side or the other. Because they are both committed to openness, they are able to tolerate shared partnerships and distribution channels. Who's to say that some day, the two Internet postage

Anne Estabrook, vice president of marketing for net.Genesis Corp., a software firm, says traditional companies are coming to realize that customers strongly prefer distribution channels that are convenient for them, regardless of how convenient, or not, those channels are for the companies doing the delivering.

"The question is, 'How comprehensive a view do you want about your customer base?'

"You need to find out which channels customers prefer for different types of transactions so you can tailor your service offering to what's most important to the customers."

companies won't find some common ground, like Solutia and its Envera allies?

Open-mindedness is not:

- Violating confidentiality,
- Tacitly dividing up the market,
- Colluding,
- Partnering with so many companies that you can't adequately follow through on your deals.

To the Starbelly team, open-mindedness is a tool. It's a competitive asset—if a competitor is not open-minded, we feel we are stronger. Staying open puts us in the best possible position to capture the best new products, services, marketing ideas and distribution channels for our customers. **Open mindedness delivers its own rewards.**

Biz Dev Buzz: When you are open, you are open to good ideas from anyone, so you are likely to get good ideas from everyone.

Case study: Student Advantage and Edu.com

"One right and honest definition of business is mutual helpfulness."
—William Feather

Student Advantage offers college kids advice, news, and a membership card that gets them major discounts at brick-and-mortar stores around the country. Edu.com, a pure Internet play going after the same kids, sells high-tech gear, books, credit cards, and bank services online, at special student rates set up by companies who want to hook students for life, with low prices now. Both companies compete for the same consumers, and both depend on proving to vendors that they have made sure a member is a genuine student.

Biz Dev brought them together. In November 1999, Student Advantage made a $4.5 million equity investment in Edu.com, put Edu.com on their home page, and placed their boss on the Edu.com Board of Directors. Meanwhile, Edu.com became Student Advantage's exclusive technology partner, for $2 million over two years, getting referrals directly from the Student Advantage home page, and urging students to become members of Student Advantage.

Working together instead of competing, the two partners now offer marketers a large student-only population, tempt universities (and their internal credit card agencies) with the combined potential for huge outsourced sales, and give students deep discounts online and off. Seems obvious when you click through the sites, but it took Biz Dev to open both companies up to the opportunity.

Stay non-exclusive (most of the time)

One of our Starbelly Biz Dev folks was going hot and heavy after the sports Web site market in the fall of 1999. Every site wanted an exclusive deal—Dunk.net, MVP.com, ActiveUSA. com, and others. But he hung tough.

Why would we lock up our ability to get at the whole sports market from the angle of each of these online retailers? He asked them, "What if Disney.com comes down the pike in

Exclusive:
Autonomous,
single, not shared
with others,
separate,
incompatible,
select, chic,
expensive, solo.

six months and I have to say, 'Sorry, we can't do that, because we've got an exclusive deal?'"

That helped them understand that it just wasn't feasible for us. We needed to spread around our risk. Sure enough, not all of these sites survived, so we were glad to have deals with several different retailers.

When the Internet hit, tech companies were already in the forefront of **non-exclusivity**. There was no way that they could know which of the companies that were clamoring for their services would end up being the winners in their particular marketplaces. So they established a lot of non-exclusive partnerships. That's why companies like Ariba, Oracle, and Akamai have rosters of partner companies that include many direct competitors.

Subsequent start-ups, looking to communicate their presence and services as quickly as possible through as many channels as possible, latched onto the idea of non-exclusivity. After all, even very fast-growing start-ups can't provide a huge menu of services to their customers. From the customer's point of view, it's preferable to deal with a start-up that recognizes its limitations and is willing to bring a rich selection of partner-provided services to the relationship. Even if the start-up's intention is to compete eventually with some of those partners (and, in the process, lose them as partners), it's better to cultivate customer loyalty from the start than to be a limited-shop stop.

Playing with
exclusivity is play-
ing with fire.

Biz Dev Buzz: Being first, and making your partners rich, locks those partners in far better than exclusivity could.

Case study: Intuit

Since 1984, Intuit Corp. has defined the market for home and small business financial software through its products Quicken and QuickBooks. In 1998, Intuit's executives decided to move toward an Internet model for many of the services included in its two flagship products, even though that might eventually cannibalize some of the sales of its shrink-wrapped software. They have found many willing partners. Since 1998, Intuit has collaborated with top-drawer partners to offer small businesses access to working capital, investment services, postage, insurance, printing, and other services, through the Quickbooks Internet gateway.

To pull people to its site, Intuit lined up alliances with at least twelve marquee portals that serve small businesses and consumers, including AOL, Excite At Home, Kinko's, and Wal-Mart. Intuit has revenue-sharing contracts with many of its service and marketing partners.

In 1998, NetLedger.com was formed with the intent of providing a set of integrated services that would have the same combined value as Intuit's constellation of partners.

Launched in fall 1999, NetLedger has already gained thirty partnerships—but none of Intuit's partners has chosen to also join forces with NetLedger.

"A standalone object, no matter how well designed, has limited potential....

"A connected object, one that is a node in a network that interacts in some way with other nodes, can give birth to a hundred unique relationships that it never could do while unconnected.

"A network is a possibility factory...."
—Kevin Kelly, *New Rules for the New Economy*

Make a bigger pie with your competition

> "We're at a stage now where there's a transformation of the economic infra-structure. It's too big a problem for any one company to solve. So you cooperate to create value."
> —Barry J. Nalebuff, Yale School of Management

Nike, Adidas, and Puma hate each other. They battle each other for shelf space, market share, sales.

But when Major League Soccer was getting started, the three brands worked together to help out, with substantial capital contributions. They made the pie bigger, instead of trying to steal someone else's slice. Without colluding, they were able to collaborate in this one area, for everyone's benefit. Without their **joint effort**, Major League Soccer might never have been created. Because of their joint efforts, they now have a new professional league to wear their uniforms.

In the old days you competed head to head, total war. Now you focus on what really differentiates you from your competitors, and look to collaborate in other areas. GM, Ford, and Daimler Chrysler will still beat each other up on car design, but they all save money pooling their purchasing info in Covisint. That's what Biz Dev offers—finesse.

Case Study: Furniture allies

> *Biz Dev finesse:* Turning a competi-tor into a sometime partner, for mutual benefit.

Take two companies that offer competing solutions for the same problem: filling an empty office with chairs, desks and cubicles. One company leases, the other sells—the same products. How could these two companies become allies?

CORT Furniture Rental **leases** office furniture across the United States. Recently, CORT chose to partner with NextOffice.com, an online business that **sells** office furniture. Together, customers will be able to lease or buy furniture at the NextOffice.com site.

At first glance, you might think that CORT is shooting itself in the caster. But because the expanded site offers both leasing and buying, chances are much greater that target customers will find the site: the combo site is simply a **larger presence** in the space.

On the NextOffice.com site, the Rental Center tab welcomes visitors to the CORT Furniture Rental pitch.

Individually, CORT and NextOffice.com are competitors—after all, customers will buy or lease only one set of office furniture. A sale to CORT is a sale that NextOffice specifically did not get.

But both companies realize that not all customers will buy, and not all customers will lease. By partnering, they each stand a better chance of capturing the customers who quickly turn away from the other's site. Customers who come to NextOffice looking to lease furniture will immediately land in CORT's lap.

CORT is in the right place to capture the attention of people who are looking to get some kind of furniture in their offices *now*.

The end result: a much greater chance that each company will gain customers from the other's leftovers.

Case Study: Staples

Ariba's e-commerce software cuts out middlemen by putting customers directly in touch with manufacturers.

So what is the office supply store, Staples—one of those middlemen—doing partnering up with Ariba?

Staples entered the Web in November 1998—almost a year after rival Office Depot. Staples was eager to catch up. In 1999, Staples made a joint marketing agreement with Ariba, to include the Staples catalog in Ariba's software package, in a bid to reach Ariba's customers directly. Staples made similar agreements with two other procurement software vendors—Commerce One, and Intelisys-Electronic Commerce.

When you unleash Biz Dev you get opportunities—and competitors— you cannot know in advance.

John Mahoney, CFO of Staples, told the *Wall Street Journal,* "In the world of the Internet, you never know—**your friends can be your enemies, and your enemies can be your friends.**"

Then, to expand the services provided on its site, Staples took a small stake in DSL.net, so it can offer visitors an easy way to sign up for a digital suscriber line. Each pass-through visitor who actually subscribes earns Staples a small fee.

Staples also invested $7 million in Register.com, and then, as part owner, got the e-mail addresses of a million businesses that registered their domain names through Register.com. E-mails go out to those businesses advertising specials, providing tips, waving the flag.

Now, as the Staples site morphs into a business service center, other Internet access companies and other domain registrars may become their new competitors.

Case Study: FedEx

Two years ago, the United States Post Office took off after FedEx in a bunch of attack ads. Today these competitors are talking about a deal. FedEx might deliver all Priority and Express Mail in the United States, while the Post Office would take slower packages and deliver them in rural areas, where there aren't a lot of customers for FedEx's overnight services.

William Henderson, who's the Postmaster General, started the deal rolling in talks with Frederick W. Smith, founder and CEO of FedEx. Henderson said, "FedEx really has some infrastructure that we need, and we have some infrastructure that they need."

How will FedEx differentiate its own service from the U.S. mail? How will the Post Office modify its traditional refusal to let delivery services into the building? Nobody knows. Issues like these are to be determined, in the fuzzy way of Biz Dev.

But both sides know one thing: **combining could help them compete better** against the kingpin of all ground deliveries, United Parcel Service.

In fact, a UPS spokesperson told the *Wall Street Journal*, "From a public policy standpoint, **this is like having the Department of Agriculture partner with McDonald's to the exclusion of Burger King.**"

Once a pure government monopoly, the Post Office has already made smaller deals with Airborne, for some home deliveries out of local post offices, with DHL for two-day deliveries to Europe, and with Emery for moving Priority Mail and making joint deliveries from businesses to consumers.

In the non-exclusive club of Biz Dev, the Post Office may soon be talking to UPS, despite the hurt feelings on both sides.

Let alliances redefine your business

A little Biz Dev can change your whole business plan.

Don't wait for a partner that's a perfect 10. Dance with the 7s, 8s and 9s.

We've seen companies change business models half a dozen times in two years, and we love it. Most people say, "It looks haphazard." But I think it shows intelligence, the essence of Biz Dev.

When we started Starbelly, the promotional products business had a fragmented supply chain. Products went from the manufacturer to a decorator, who shipped them to a distributor, who sold them to the customer. We wanted to change the dynamics of the supply chain, infusing technology to make it more efficient, and allowing each player in the supply chain to realize new productivity enhancements.

Early on we formed alliances with one of the largest distributors, and one of the largest decorators, and then we said to both of them, what if the decorator moved inside the distributor's warehouse, which is gigantic—it has hundreds of copies of every item right on the shelves. Instead of shipping a golf shirt here and there, over the space of a week or so, let's put the decorator in the same four walls as the inventory, to speed up reaction time. We all save on inventory, shipping time, shipping costs, availability. Those savings will mean better, cheaper, faster results for the customer. By eliminating some of the friction—cutting out almost a week—we ended up with a better supply chain, and a whole different idea of our business. Until we did Biz Dev with these partners, none of us could have envisioned this simple idea.

> "Wealth, in this new regime, flows directly from innovation, not optimization. That is, wealth is not gained by perfecting the known, but by imperfectly seizing the unknown."
> —Kevin Kelly, *New Rules for the New Economy*

Case Study: Stamps.com

Quick—what does Stamps.com sell? Stamps, you say?

Nice guess, but this fast-moving company has already morphed from a purveyor of postage via the Internet into a multi-faceted e-commerce fulfillment, logistics and shipping supplier, to a company that licenses its proprietary technology to let other companies distribute value-bearing documents (like concert tickets) through the Web and consumers' desktop printers.

What is good Biz Dev? Fast. Aggressive. Non-exclusive.

All of this has happened at lightning speed. In August 1998, Doug Walner, Senior VP of Business Development, was the fourth employee hired. Now Stamps.com has 400 employees, over $300 million in venture funding, and is already spinning off start-ups devoted to capitalizing on various technologies it has built along the way.

None of this could have happened without Biz Dev. From the moment Stamps.com was founded, **it aggressively partnered with every company it could**, ruthlessly moving in on territory that archrivals E-Stamp.com, Pitney Bowes, and Neopost thought was sewn up. Exclusive deals are great, says Walner, but he'll accept a non-exclusive deal just to get the Stamps.com logo and link slapped right up there next to the logos and links of any of the other postage-by-Internet companies. Its extensive, and growing, list of partnerships includes AOL, Microsoft, Quicken, IBM, ZDNet, Deluxe, 3M, Hotoffice, U.S. West, IBM, Lotus, Concentric…**the list never ends**.

At age thirty, with seven years' experience in Biz Dev, Walner is about as seasoned as they come. His career started with a wireless communications firm, where he got experience developing third party deals and figuring out how to get hardware manufacturers interested in his firm's wireless messaging software.

Next was a stint with a software development firm developing retail distribution channels. Then he moved early into the Internet by doing Biz Dev for a first-generation application service provider.

When he looked into Stamps.com, Walner loved what he saw—a plan to create secure software that would enable consumers and businesses to download United States Postal Service postage into their computers, and print out the right amounts, as needed, directly onto envelopes and labels.

Competitors rely on a small hardware plug-in that stores the postage. Stamps.com doesn't—making it the first completely digital delivery system for postage.

When Walner joined up, the company had nothing more than a really, really good idea. There was only the barest of software demos. Everyone knew that it would take a year to get the software built.

"It was a good time to get in there and see where we could get the strong relationships that we'll need when we launch," says Walner.

"It was very clear to me that there was a big opportunity at hand. They'd just gotten approval from the USPS to go to public pilot, which was a validation of the software. It was a chance to do something from the ground up."

Fortunately, Walner doesn't mind getting his hands dirty. He dug into the gritty details of building Stamps.com's distribution channel, which he envisioned would be mainly through partners that already had credibility with the mass audiences who could reasonably be expected to try out the downloadable stamp idea.

"We wanted to capitalize on the advantage of having a software-only solution. We didn't need to worry about retail distribution, or building products. **We had to leverage the Internet as a distribution channel for the service**," Walner explains.

"Locking up the key distribution channels on an exclusive basis was a key goal, but getting key partnerships, even on a premiere or non-exclusive market basis was critical, so in some cases we've settled for non-exclusive relationships."
—Doug Walner, Stamps. com

Walner knew that his competitors had slowed themselves down by staying wedded to the hardware/software blended service. They were distracted by getting approvals for their digital postal meters, while Stamps.com only had to worry about creating the software and a way to get the service out to people. Aggressively approaching every logical partner and taking the best available real estate ensured that Stamps.com would be nearly everywhere its competitors were—and plenty of places they weren't.

Walner went out on one very big limb—committing millions of dollars to partnership channels before the technology had received final approval from the Post Office. Stamps.com went public in June 1999 and immediately spent a big chunk of the proceeds on locking up those distribution partnerships.

The three-year relationship with America Online, for instance, is extraordinarily valuable, yet non-exclusive. "AOL is continually dropping CDs from the sky—it plans to send out a billion CDs over our three year period," says Walner. His deal with AOL cost him $56 million for that three years, but "it was cheap for us to be on that software upgrade. None of our competitors can get to that for three years," he says.

The AOL deal is already paying off; half of Stamps.com's network traffic comes from AOL. But, the credibility that AOL provided the start-up was pretty important, too. "AOL won't take just anybody's money," says Walner.

"They want to make sure you'll be successful with them. When we went with them first, they wanted a **non-exclusive relationship** because they wanted to see which of the digital postage companies would be the winner in this space. Twelve months later, we went to them with our data and test results and said, 'Look, we are going to be the major player in this industry. This will serve not just the small business but also the consumer.'"

Deals like that don't happen unless the Biz Dev staff already has a solid working relationship with the potential partner.

"It was difficult modeling when we didn't have a live service, but from what we could tell from our pilot, we would be able to get (AOL) customers for the right (acquisition) cost. If you can do that, you're meeting your strategic goals. So pull the trigger. Do the deal," he says.

Walner doesn't settle for a glorified link.

His distribution partnerships include a downloadable version of Stamps.com's service that the buyer enacts with a single click on the Stamps.com logo. Every graphic impression of Stamps.com is embedded with a way for a casual surfer to become a stamps customer immediately.

With the world's single biggest Internet service provider locked up, Walner moved on to conquer the small business world.

Plenty of upstart small biz portals would love to get Stamps.com's money, but Walner was angling for the big fish—embedded links in Intuit's universally popular personal and small business accounting software Quicken and QuickBooks.

Stamps.com is now embedded not only at Intuit's Web sites but also in the latest versions of the shrink-wrapped software itself.

> "The distributor is dead. Long live the value-added, knowledge-intensive business partner."
> —Tom Peters

And the rest of Stamps.com's long array of partners? "Everything else you see we didn't spend money on," says Walner. "Office Depot and other partners—we have some arrangements where everyone benefits by driving performance through revenue sharing."

Non-exclusive partners are taking bets on who the major players will be. "The fact that we have a pretty broad set of partners, and a lot of them, is proof that we have the best solution."

Walner adds, "Strategy trumps price. You can only put a price tag on a deal once you

Stamps.com reaches out to four different audiences with mailing and shipping solutions.

see how the strategies mesh—and where the value is added."

Clearly, investors have been impressed. In February 1999, Stamps.com raised $30 million from a consortium of venture capital firms. Its June 1999 IPO and subsequent public rounds brought in $350 million for the rest of the year. In October 1999, Stamps.com bought iShip.com to extend its reach into the small business market by providing shipping, fulfillment and logistics services. Since launching the service in October 1999, Stamps.com has won more than 200,000 paying customers.

Test the limits of openness

Not every permutation of neutrality will be received enthusiastically.

Governmental agencies, such as the Justice Department and state attorneys general, are well aware of the fine line between an open-to-all marketplace that is organized and underwritten by industry leaders, and a marketplace tacitly dominated by industry leaders that invites illegal collusion, price-fixing, and other market-dampening consequences.

For instance, a travel Web site that was being organized in mid-2000 by five of the biggest U.S. airlines was barely public knowledge before it was being slammed by travel agents and other travel Web sites as anti-competitive and illegal.

Open mindedness is a **tool** for business development, not an overriding philosophy that obliterates common sense.

Just because theoretically you can partner with anyone doesn't mean that you should.

Some companies have bad track records of following through on their Biz Dev deals—they don't do what they promised, or don't do it well.

Others may make a deal and then turn around and undermine the spirit of it by cutting you out of a desirable alliance that should have included you.

Avoid these companies. Your reputation will be *dragged down* with theirs.

Many alliances just won't make sense, at least not obvious sense. Scrutinize deals from the perspective of your customers before you commit.

Will this partnership confuse them, send conflicting messages to the market about what your mission and core competencies are?

Figure out another way to work with a company that offers value, but will dilute your corporate image if you partner. There's no www.Kmart.com. Plug that into your URL and you land at www.bluelight.com— K-Mart's online alter ego.

Bluelight sells things and services, and it is heavily cross-marketed through K-Mart's traditional advertising avenues. But it might be confusing to K-Mart's core market if BlueLight pretended that K-Mart online was a literal interpretation of the real-world K-Mart.

So K-Mart has created a sister site that can blend K-Mart's retailing expertise with the strengths of e-commerce.

Is K-Mart doing this alone?

K-Mart distinguishes its brick-and-mortar stores from its Web site, leaving only a tiny logo at the top.

No. It's partnering with Softbank Venture Capital. That affiliation gave the sister site a real boost.

We got pretty far down the road with an entertainment company before we realized that part of their overall business plan was also to set up a structure for private-label stores. They wanted to do stores, we already did stores—it looked like we were squaring off as competitors.

Then we realized that our point of commonality was that they could use Starbelly as a supplier.

We agreed that we'd be one of their suppliers where there's no conflict, and in markets where we're direct competitors, we would not bad-mouth each other.

Your marketing message must be stronger and more consistent than ever when you are imaginative and barrier-breaking about your affiliations.

Find points of commonality— they get conversations started.

"In this new century, success will go to the companies that partner their way to a new future, not those that put heavy assets onto their balance sheets."

—*Business Week*

To some degree, your partners and affiliates define your identity.

If you have a diverse group of affiliations, you must work extra hard to help your target market make sense of them. Oracle's slogan is "Oracle Software Powers the Internet."

That clears things up for anyone who wonders, "Is Oracle all about databases? or customer service? or enterprise software?"

The answer is "All of the above."

Finally, don't underestimate the impact of an exclusive deal—the more high profile the partner and the more it forces your competition into a little corner of the market, the better.

Biz Dev Buzz: When you land alliances that are worth the exclusivity, set off the fireworks.

Check it out

To learn more about the Webified gas stations planned at BP Amoco, see **http://www.bp.com**

To watch the automakers build their collaborative supply site, visit **http://www.covisint.com**

If you're a student, get deep discounts, and watch the ties to Student Advantage, at **http://www.edu.com**. Then look at the space their partners give Edu.com, at **http://www.studentadvantage.com**

If you're into chemicals, sealants or adhesives, see how a clearinghouse handles business-to-business transactions at **http://www.envera.com**

With a few big partners, E-Stamp squares off against its rivals, at **http://www.estamp.com**.

Look at all the partners of Stamps.com, at **http://www. stamps.com/company/partners/**

Hey, come visit our home site for custom-branded merchandise, and a glimpse of lots of our partners, at **http://www.halo.com**

Partnering with just about everyone who deals with small business, you have the brilliant Intuit, at **http://www.intuit.com/corporate/ pressroom/partner_releases.html**

Watch how you're directed to the blue light specials, at K-Mart's site, **http:// www.kmart.com**

To see how fast the airlines' joint site is taking off, see **http://www.orbitz.com**

Partners, communities, events, and customer success stories—Oracle posts several new ones every day, at **http://www.oracle.com**

To see the way the partnership with Cort Furniture works, check out the Next Office's tab for the Rental Center, at **http:// www.nextoffice.com**

To see how Staples expanded its offerings through partners, see **http://www.staples.com**

For the King Kong of package and mail delivery, see **http://www.usps.gov**

Take Biz Dev to the next level!
Join us at **http://www.BizDev3.com** for other resources, ongoing conversation, and the BizDev3.0 newsletter.

Step 3: Speed + simplicity = success

How fast can you go?

Are you happy when you can cut the number of committee approvals for a new alliance from five to three?

You're not fast enough.

Are you thrilled when your well-timed temper tantrums get Legal off its duff to sign off on your pending deals in only two weeks?

You're not fast enough.

Are you pleased when you get to the *Industry Standard* when it's only two weeks old, find a company with a mission that intersects with your company's, and call them within a week of clipping the article?

You're not fast enough.

Speed is fun for its own sake, but your company will only grow when you get into fifth gear. Only when you are fast will you arrive **first** to claim a rich stake of market. **New markets are defined by the swift who arrive there first and can cast everyone else as an also-ran.**

Market innovators are not necessarily the biggest companies, or the ones with the most products or customers. They are the ones that are quickest to draw on customers' **unarticulated needs** and shape their products to anticipate and meet those needs.

In this chapter:

Strip it down to speed it up

Line up the sacred cows and shoot them

Die, committee, die

Ready, set, deal

The importance of getting there first

Announce that you are first

Be the first to redefine an existing market

Measure your speed

"The Internet is a tool, and the biggest impact of that tool is speed. The speed of actions, the speed of deliberations, and the speed of information have all increased, and will continue to increase."

—Andy Grove, CEO, Intel

General Electric's Aircraft Engine division wanted to get a business-to-business e-commerce system up fast. Working with SpaceWorks, Inc., they created an online commerce space for new and existing customers and firms that maintain the engines.

They pulled it off in **eight weeks flat**. That's fast. Maintenance managers don't have to wonder anymore how to connect with the Aircraft Engine division through the Internet.

At Starbelly, speed has been at the essence of the company. We know that plenty of people in our industry have great marketing ideas, and certainly can conceive of a better way of doing business. But we felt that our vision, combined with the agility of the Internet, presented an opportunity. The missing link was the execution itself, and we never lost sight of speed as central to our execution.

General Electric's Aircraft Engine Web site

Biz Dev Buzz: When you move faster than you thought possible, you get **more customers**. That kind of speed leads to greater revenues, which builds credibility with new and existing customers—and investors.

We approached the venture capital community with the same sense of speed that we had in our attack on the promotional products industry. When we went to raise our first round of venture capital, our guiding principle was speed, not valuation. Our first round of venture capital was $1.5 million, but the import of that round was the fact that it was closed. We were able to build on that momentum as we began our relationship with Chase Capital Partners and Flatiron Partners, two very high-profile venture capital firms. Both Chase Capital and Flatiron appreciated our urgency, and their subsequent $8 million investment shortly after the $1.5 million investment gave us the funding we needed to execute our business. It was not the amount of these investments that made the difference in Starbelly's success—rather, it was the speed of the investments, and the fact that capital raising was a part of our speed, not an obstacle to it.

> "Everything should be made as simple as possible, but not simpler."
> —Albert Einstein

Strip it down to speed it up

The cleaner the design, the faster the ride. Think race-cars, rockets, Speedo swimsuits.

Eliminate anything that compromises speed—ruthlessly.

Focus on your purpose and why it is important to get to market fast, and you begin to realize that your company has to make some sacrifices to achieve the goal. You may not be able to fit some old vendors, suppliers or distributors into your plans. Maybe they are too slow to respond, they don't understand your purpose, or their products don't fit the market you are gunning for. If they are going to exert too much drag, you must tell them they can't come along for the rocket ride.

Be ruthless, too, when looking at potential new alliances and partnerships. Many good companies and people and products will almost fit. Reject them.

If a relationship is going to confuse, muddy, fuzz up, or complicate your customers' understanding of what your value is to them, it is going to slow you down, because:

"Space and time have become elastic media that expand or contract at will. Global financial markets respond to news in an instant. Nonstop software projects 'follow the sun' around the world each day."
—Don Tapscott, David Ticoll, and Alex Lowy, *Digital Capital*

- You will be **stuck** explaining it to customers in long press releases and brochures and Web site cul-de-sacs.

- Your other partners will be **confused**: what is the point of this alliance?

- You will be sending **conflicting and confusing** images internally—your process of choosing what fits and what doesn't will appear arbitrary, discouraging employees who get it and further muddling those who don't. Your company will be awash in irrelevant ideas, and it will be your fault.

Everyone on the Biz Dev team must understand that there is no room for scope creep when it comes to finding the right partnerships and alliances. Others in your company will see the excitement and energy thrown off by the Biz Dev team, and they may start pushing for their own projects, clients, customers, suppliers and vendors to get in on what you're doing. "We've gotta get Joe's Semiconductors on our Web site! They've been such great suppliers!"

Don't kid yourself. Joe and his semiconductors, as wonderful as they both are, are still suppliers. If nothing has dramatically changed about Joe's company or if his semiconductors do not materially change what you deliver to your customers, it would be a grave error to recast Joe as a partner. Doing so would blunt the impact of Biz Dev and make it just another stupid vendor-recognition program. Don't let others in your company hijack Biz Dev for their own purposes.

Speed is much easier to achieve if your vision is simple.

If you burden a deal with all kinds of reporting requirements, testing and other junk, the deal gets so bulky it takes forever to get it approved—never mind enacted. Free the deal from extraneous complications and you can zero in on its essence.

Reduce paperwork as much as possible to enhance speed.

Do the same with Biz Dev reporting structures—aim for fewer, more meaningful approvals rather than a lot of rubber-stamping.

The pace of technological change is not going to slow down. The rush to the Internet by consumers and companies is not just some odd blip on an analyst's historical timeline. **Things are not going back to 'normal.'** No matter what industry you're in, the technology is changing at a pace that keeps accelerating—faster and faster. You can't stop the car and you can't get out. But why would you want to? Once you have mastered speed through Biz Dev, you will never hit the brakes again.

Biz Dev Buzz: Fast is now normal.

Line up the sacred cows and shoot them

Careful long-term planning just won't work. Committee meetings? Forget it. Waiting for sacred cows like these to get out of the way will just slow you down.

I hear some companies saying, "We would rather be best than first. We would rather wait, and get it right, and *then* make our big splash."

That's **old-economy thinking**. It reeks. Here's why.

Companies that think that way are counting on the market to pace itself to their development process. Somehow, they are deluding themselves into thinking that their customers are just **assuming** that they, great omniscient companies, are going to sail in with perfect solutions—a perfect tech service, or perfect product. That's not the way it works.

First, most customers **won't wait**.

Customers usually interpret silence as ignorance. If you had something to say about how a process or product could be better, you'd say it—right? It doesn't matter whether you're keeping quiet because you don't care or just don't have a better idea—either way, the customers are stuck without a solution.

"When Federal Express entered the marketplace, the older parcel-delivery services were baffled by the high prices it proposed to charge. The traditional pricing models were based on just two variables: weight and size. Speed, anyone?"

—James Gleick, *Faster*

A competitor of yours will come along with a solution and even if it seems to you half-baked and flawed, it's better than your perfection-in-process, which is locked in your top-secret lab somewhere.

For instance, in 2000, fulfillment became one of the hottest topics of concern for e-commerce companies. The headaches of keeping up with demand during the 1999 holiday selling season forced many to realize that they absolutely had to find better ways to get the goods out of the warehouse and into the hands of customers.

Of course, start-up firms were already rushing to fill the void. One, NextJet, has created software that instantly figures out the most efficient way to get a package from here to there, often on the same day, using already existing package-delivery services.

In mid-2000, NextJet was starting to line up partners. It had plenty of funding, the technology, and a great idea, and it was gradually lining up e-commerce site partners. As word gets out about its service through its early partners, such as b2bstores.com, customers may begin to wonder, why can't I get same-day delivery at every site? Do the other sites assume that I don't even want to be offered the option?

Perhaps e-commerce sites that don't partner with NextJet are reserving judgment and want to see how it works out before they commit. Meanwhile, retail sites that do want to signal to their customers that they know urgency sometimes overcomes price, can differentiate themselves from the pack by offering delivery via NextJet.

"The central economic imperative of the industrial age was to increase productivity.... But today productivity is a nearly meaningless **byproduct** in the network economy.

"The central economic imperative of the network economy is to **amplify relationships**."
—Kevin Kelly,
New Rules for the New Economy

The NextJet site.

Partnering with cutting-edge new services may be less risky than you think, if you are also leveraging the fact of the partnership for marketing purposes.

As the service catches on with sites, it will become less noteworthy and more subject to commodity pricing. **Only early partners will have reaped the benefit of associating with an innovative new service**.

Customers who are working to squeeze inefficiencies out of their markets and processes are going to go for an **imperfect solution** on the theory that they can work with the supplier who recognizes their special needs to help make the solution right.

In fact, such customers might even welcome the chance to tweak first and second editions, figuring that they will then get a product that fits their particular needs better.

That commitment binds them to the supplier, who not only indicated that it cared about their problem, but also made them part of the solution by inviting them to be part of fine-tuning it.

By the time your product rolls out, it's to the sound of one hand clapping. Nobody cares, because your customers' loyalty is locked up elsewhere. And of course, you're assuming that you've been able to incorporate changing technological standards into your product along the way, which is nearly impossible to do. Not only is your product obsolete when you introduce it, but you've got precious few customers and partners to help you leapfrog it ahead of the competition for the next release or version.

Convinced yet? Secrecy suffocates. Speed frees, because, among other things, it gives out advance signals of your intentions to your customers and your competitors.

Just ask Hewlett-Packard. It sat back in the late 1990s while Sun Microsystems moved in and dominated the market for Internet hardware. In May 2000, HP finally won a huge high-profile Internet account—it landed an enormous contract to upgrade Amazon.com's back-room operations. But it took three months of negotiations to prevail over pitches made by Sun, Compaq, and other competitors. HP desperately needed a blockbuster Internet client for bragging rights. "Hey, we're in the game, we're back, Amazon chose us!"

Or ask Rand McNally. It only got Biz Dev religion in late 1999—more than three years after MapQuest started collaborating with Web site developers, software developers and just

> Sacred cows: Stupid processes, committees that have subcommittees, hierarchies that result in stagnation, legal minutia, and documentation for no good reason.

> "It's important to be fast, but it's also important to be fast for the right customers."
> —David Bovet, Mercer Management Consulting

about everybody else to place its maps on their Web sites and in their software. With new executive leadership, Rand McNally has vowed to make up the lost ground. Meanwhile, MapQuest continues to leap ahead by having its maps embedded in the latest version of Oracle e-commerce software. MapQuest is an integral part of some of the most popular e-commerce software in the world, getting a Biz Dev-negotiated free ride onto probably thousands of Web sites. It's no wonder that MapQuest is becoming synonymous with interactive, Internet-based mapping systems.

As the business-to-business e-commerce market approaches 42 percent of all non-service transactions by 2005, you can't be sure which particular models will survive. Instead, you have to move quickly to affiliate with several diverse models to spread the risk and increase your chances of being in on a winning formula.

Source: Jupiter Communications

If you have ever heard people complaining of these **speed bumps**, your company is probably not moving as fast as it could:

- "Things are stuck in committee."
- "Our customer base trusts us to come up with the right solution, not just a quick solution."
- "We can only move as fast as our customers (or vendors or suppliers) do."
- "The technology isn't where we want it to be. We'll wait for the next generation."
- "The board doesn't get it."

The old fable of the tortoise and the hare is being rewritten. This time, the hare wins.

Case Study: EqualFooting

In May 1999, three ex-McKinsey managers came up with the idea for a supply super-site for small businesses in the manufacturing and construction industries.

By January 2000, they were open for business and had over thirty marketing partnerships either consummated or in process. In the suddenly crowded category, Chief Business Development Officer Aaron Martin knew that EqualFooting.com had to push ahead as fast as possible to get its message out to customers.

"People say that start-ups are so 'chicken and egg.' There's no egg!" he says. **"You have to build the product with the partners first.** You can't expect the buyers to come and open up the request-for-proposal process without a catalog."

EqualFooting got its chicken with a roster of creative marketing and distribution alliances, including the Small Business Administration, BankOne/First USA, Automatic Data Processing, Freightquote.com and several small and women contractors' associations.

What new markets and customers could your company win if it got products to market twice as fast as it does now?

What ground would you have gained if you had responded to certain opportunities 50 percent faster?

The EqualFooting site

As we were setting up our first Starbelly alliances, we knew that we had to persuade big customers not just to invest money, but also to shift their existing custom-products business over to us. We had to start executing our concept simultaneously with the build-up of operations and the technology infrastructure.

So, we leveraged **our existing relationships** with major customers. We got cash from them immediately as we processed orders for shirts and hats in the old-world way (at that point, our order fulfillment functions were up and running), and we were able to use their credibility as a wedge with other potential customers that were just as big.

Die, committee, die

Once we get hold of a great idea, we do not sit on it.

Right away, we talk as long as we can with the partner, exploring as many possibilities and details as reasonable in a first conversation:

A good rule of thumb is that it should take about seven working days to complete an agreement for a marketing alliance.

- What resources can your company dedicate to this collaboration?
- How much of your core market is represented in the segment that intersects with our market?
- What are you looking for in this partnership—revenue, market share, distribution, something else? Here's what would make this work for us.
- Can we agree on terms that are beneficial to our mutual customers, and both companies?

Sometimes this takes all of ten minutes. Occasionally, it takes less.

One deal cut by a VP of Business Development at Starbelly took all of five minutes. She was on her way out the door to a meeting, so she told the guy, "Look, let's make it easy. Let's decide on what we have in common and what we want to do together, so we can start working together." So that's what they did.

We aren't unique. I have never met a company that is successful at Biz Dev that sends potential deals into endless committee meetings. You have to have some meetings—you need some quick due diligence and you need to ensure buy-in from the departments in your company that will have to collaborate directly with the new partner to make the deal a reality for your customers. Still, the single best way to kill a deal is to put it into queue for review.

The nature of committees is groupthink. That's why they exist—so that everyone can share the responsibility (and try to hog the glory) for the results.

So much Biz Dev already involves consensus: that you have a shared vision, that you can enact it in a certain way, by a certain date, and extract certain results from that. People who are good at Biz Dev see that in flash. The why is obvious to them. It's the how that takes time—hammering out enough details so that the implementation team knows what it needs to do to enact the deal, and that the executives know what you've committed the company to do.

Yahoo, that master of Biz Dev, makes **an average of two or three new alliances every week**—so many that it can't even announce them all with fanfare. Each deal takes five to ten hours of negotiation time.

PriceWaterhouse Coopers and the Conference Board found that e-biz accounted for less than 5 percent of revenues for 70 percent of the companies they surveyed. That might be due to the rudimentary nature of those e-businesses: only 28 percent could process transactions through their sites; 40 percent could receive orders electronically; 60 percent didn't have extranets linking them to key suppliers and financial partners.

Some Yahoo partners

Biz Dev Buzz: If you can't figure out what you want to do together in ten hours, then forget it. Agree to let the idea percolate for a few days or weeks and then talk again.

Ready, set, deal

To avoid wasting time in your first meeting with a potential partner, do your homework ahead of time.

That's what Denise Brousseau recommends. She spent several years doing Biz Dev for Motorola, then co-founded the Forum for Women Entrepreneurs, of which she is President.

"Save yourself the heartache of a bad match," she says.

"The worst mistake is to send a Biz Dev person out there (to do a deal) and then have

"Companies that are successful will have cultures that thrive on change, even though change makes most people very uncomfortable. In the end, you might just have speed, talent, and branding. Those things may be the only differentiators."
—John Chambers, CEO, Cisco

the CEO say, 'Why would we partner with them? I'd never choose them.'"

Doing your competitive intelligence will save you from wasting time, energy and goodwill because you won't be running after potential partners that don't jibe with your company's mission and objectives.

"Your first job is to sit down with the powers that be within your company and find out what they think a good partner looks like," she says. "The more homework you can do to define your perfect partner—the ideal company to compliment yours—the better. To make the deal, what do they (the potential partner) have to give, what do you give, what do they give up and what do you give up? The more thinking you do about that before you walk out the door, the more effective you'll be."

The culture, not the executives, is the main ingredient determining the flavor of a company's Biz Dev.

For instance, your company might define a likely ally as:

- A company that gives yours prestige because you're affiliating with them

- A company that offers a product, service, distribution channel or something else that you can't build in-house fast enough for your market penetration plans

- A company that has the proven ability to implement the partnership, given the company's track record in Biz Dev and general corporate operational history

Anyone in Biz Dev who's worth his salt

can figure out within a few minutes of opening a discussion with a potential partner if there's chemistry there or not, says Brousseau. "If they're eager to go ahead, and you're setting up lunch, and they want to introduce you to others, that's it. But if they just say, 'Thanks for the meeting,' then the deal isn't going anywhere." The needs of the two companies may not be balanced enough for a partnership, or the timing to market may be off.

The relationship can still be valuable, though, if there is a meeting of minds, company cultures and company goals. "If at the end of the meeting, you're saying, 'You really ought to talk to X' and they're saying, 'You ought to talk to Y,' and you're both willing to share your Rolodexes, that means that you're both invested in the other's success and it's starting to click," she says. "Continue to cultivate those relationships to see what else you could be doing together."

Often, two CEOs who get together and strike a deal on the golf course are thrilled that they're being so decisive (and have created a good story to tell at Young Presidents' Club meetings). Maybe, maybe not, says Brousseau, who points out that most presidents only know "10 percent" of what's really going on in their companies, especially when it comes to the projects that the Biz Dev team is working on. **The best way to achieve speed in putting together deals is not by executive fiat but by creating a company culture that sets the expectation that includes everyone.**

Biz Dev Buzz: A collaborative spirit, fostered by meetings that lay the Biz Dev process open to all, increases the chances that

"Simplicity, of all things, is the hardest to be copied."
—Richard Steele

you'll gain access to contacts outside the usual
Biz Dev circles.

What to get ready

To be fast and focused, you need to have
some tools at the ready—before you pick up
the phone.

- **Know your own company's elevator
  pitch**—the one you're using today
  and the one you'll probably be using
  in a year, given current and reasonable
  growth patterns and expansions for
  your company, your industry and the
  markets you target.

- **Know your parameters for each
  kind of partnership: technical, distribution, marketing.** What does
  your company require of the other
  company, and what kind of value to
  the customer must be delivered by
  each of these types of partnerships?

- **Know how far these parameters can
  be bent.** Will you accept a quid-pro-
  quo arrangement with a distribution
  partner if you have always demanded
  revenue sharing in the past?

- **Know who on your staff is available**
  that day to answer questions, to help
  you negotiate, and to bring in the
  rubber stamp of big boss approval,
  if you need it, to seal a deal. Also
  know who you can tap in related
  departments that will have to enact
  the deal, such as IT, marketing, sales
  and production.

"There are two
options for
Internet
companies. Get
bigger fast, or get
smaller fast.
"If you're not
one of the top
three players in
any category,
eventually you'll
be eaten—or die.
That's a pretty
good incentive to
find partners that
can help you
grow."
—Kevin
O'Connor, CEO,
DoubleClick

- **Know your company's overall revenue**, profit, market share and growth **goals** so you can keep in mind how this particular deal will help you achieve those.

- **Leverage e-mail, conference calls, instant messaging and videoconferencing** as much as possible to bring in additional Biz Dev experts in your company to **keep negotiations moving along.** Don't wait for someone to come back in from the latest talked-to-death Internet conference.

- **Look for similarities** between this deal and others your company may have cut. Keep a searchable database of deals on your company intranet so you can refer back to terms and draw on the experience of the whole Biz Dev team as you put together the deal at hand.

- **Have boilerplate agreements**, company direction statements, and other confirming terminology and paperwork at your fingertips so you can push them to the other party even as you're on the phone.

- **When you click with someone, don't let go.** If it's obvious that you both see significant value in a partnership, and just as obvious that it will take more than one phone conversation to iron out the agreement, collect lots of detail on the company, its goals and targets for the deal, the terms, and contact information. Don't hang up

"Everyone on the Net is scrambling to get big fast. We did five acquisitions and three strategic investments in less than a year. There's a clear sense that speed is a necessity."
—Bob Davis, CEO, Lycos

until you've got all that sitting on your screen in front of you.

Case Study: Purchase Pro

PurchasePro.com is making speed its business.

Originally launched in March 1997, Purchase Pro is a service that enables small businesses to compete for work from large companies, and to buy the materials, goods and services they need for their own operations.

By spring 2000, PurchasePro had gotten so good at running e-marketplaces that it reformulated its software in order to license it for private-label use to distributors, corporate procurement departments, and market-makers.

The guarantee is that the software suite will enable a marketplace to be created from nothing to operational in forty-five days flat.

PurchasePro can only make that promise because it has smoothed out the glitches from its system over the course of creating 155 co-branded systems, many for partners like AOL, Office Depot, and IBM. By getting heavy-hitter partners early in the game, PurchasePro has fueled an upward spiral of credibility, attracting additional name-brand companies. That critical mass helped attract the 23,000 (and counting) small and medium-sized companies to the PurchasePro database, which in turn makes the service more valuable to the buyers, and so on and so on.

"Anybody who's been assigned profit-and-loss objectives can understand the value of a good Biz Dev team," says Jeff Anderson, Senior

Partners can provide an early-warning system for both dangers and opportunities as companies strive to respond to their customers in real time. That means that companies must realize that their ability to collect data from third parties, integrate it with their own data, and quickly analyze it and communicate direction throughout the enterprise will be a critical skill.

Source: Forrester Research, Inc.

VP of Sales and Strategic Development for PurchasePro. "It's easy to lie awake at night and worry about getting new revenue streams. The biggest challenge is making sure that all that work is tied to the core strategy of the business. A lousy Biz Dev team is always cutting deals that don't have a prayer of being integrated into the product. Many Biz Dev teams have fantastic ideas, but they don't think about how it will get integrated."

Simplicity is the essence of success when letting the Biz Dev team cut loose to run after new products and channels.

"Make sure the team has a strong understanding of the company channel, of its weaknesses and strengths. Make sure that Biz Dev works closely with the existing sales and marketing team. They are there to grow the company, but they also have to be tied into the current company to bring value (from the deals they cut)."

At the same time, Anderson cautions against becoming engrossed with one-shot deals that probably will bring in a rush of revenues, but don't have much, if any, long-term benefit for the company's strategic direction.

When he was with a telco, Anderson was constantly approached by people who wanted to leverage the company's mailings, bills, and other marketing channels to sell products that superficially made sense—modems, headsets, call center software and the like.

"It was complementary in terms of communications, but our model of monthly services didn't fit," he says.

"You can't sell everything through one

channel, but these companies were always expecting us to be a sales channel for them. There wasn't a mutual advantage for us, or if there was, it wasn't big enough to justify the relationship." And that doesn't even begin to factor in the hassle that his salespeople would have had explaining the gear and software to the telco customers, and confusions with support and the implied endorsements.

To help his Biz Dev staff focus, focus, focus, on strategy and long-term payoff, Anderson makes sure they understand the platform, players and infrastructure of both PurchasePro and its customers.

"If you don't define it up front, it's doomed to failure," he says.

"The problem is, when you put someone in the Biz Dev role without the skills (of understanding the big picture and what it takes to deliver the back end of the deal), they'll gravitate back to the skills they know—such as sales. And that's what they'll do."

The Purchase Pro site

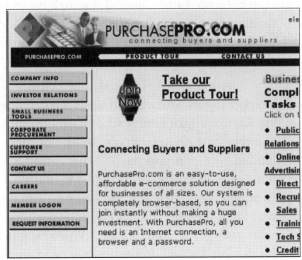

Caution from Andy Grove

When *Business Week* breathlessly asked
Andy Grove, CEO of Intel, what he thought
about the speed of transactions in the E-conomy,
he pointed out that the gating item is your
people.

"This business about speed has its limits.
Brains don't speed up. The **exchange of ideas**
doesn't really speed up, only the overhead that
slowed down the exchange....

"You can reach people around the clock,
but they won't think any better or any faster just
because you've reached them faster. The **give
and take** remains a limiting factor."

The importance of getting there first

In Biz Dev, speed is only worth the effort if
it parachutes you into your customers' territory
before your competitors get there.

Your mission is to figure out what your
customers need and want and, through business
development, marshal the resources to create the
products and services they need—and deliver
them before your competitors do.

Getting there **first** opens up the chance to
develop loyalty among your customers. Other
attractive companies may set foot on the beach
the very next day, but if you are the one who
landed first and approached the customers,
with your value proposition and determination
to serve them, then you are going to get the
benefit of the doubt when customers consider
who will get their business. The guy who
introduces himself second may be charming

and credible and have resources, but he is serving leftovers.

Customers have already heard this same value proposition—from you.

And if you have managed to establish a shred, a crumb, of credibility, customers will feel honor-bound to consider anything you have to say along with what the second-arriver says.

Customers don't know you well, but they know you one day better than the other guy. And the third guy to arrive? He has to wave his arms and jump up and down and advertise on the SuperBowl and air-drop $10 gift certificates to get the customers' attention. Customers already have two perfectly reasonable options, and one of them was smart enough to be first.

Started in 1993, eCredit.com became operational in June 1999 with the aim of enabling businesses to get loans, immediately, online. Barely a year later, it had lined up multiple technology partners (who committed to integrate eCredit into their products) and several major consulting and distribution channel alliances. One of its partners, its first bank, First Union, landed in May 2000. Why didn't banks come up with this idea themselves? It's hard to imagine that someone at some bank somewhere didn't imagine this scenario. But eCredit moved rapidly to become integrated with the software companies that would carry its services to the end users, instead of assuming that the end users would turn to their local banks for an instant online business loan service.

eCredit is an appealing partner because it offers services that make it easier for a customer

Be sure that your partners don't cannibalize each other, especially if you have set up revenue-sharing agreements with them.

"We're big fans of handing out offers with a fuse attached. If you don't commit within 12 hours, this deal blows up. We want each deal to happen fast. We don't want to give the other company time to talk with our competitors."
—Bo Peabody, Lycos

to buy its partners' services. One could argue that the individual impact of partners offering services through an e-commerce site is diminished as the total number of partners goes up. Indirectly, they may compete with each other for incremental spending: hmm, what will it be: a fancy, four-color printed direct mail campaign or a new copier/fax machine?

But no matter what other products or services are offered, eCredit complements them perfectly because it enables the customer to pay for anything. A customer can have the mail campaign *and* the copier/fax if she qualifies for and gets a small loan from eCredit while shopping online. eCredit shrewdly offers a service that its partners can't get anywhere else—instant, real-time information about a credit applicant's credit history and likelihood of repaying the debt completely, and on time. In this way they help buyers and sellers close a transaction in minutes.

When you move fast like this, you aren't just impressing yourself and the people in your company. **You are saying to your customers: you are so important to us that we will not stop searching until we have found the right combination of resources, inside our company and outside, to make your life easier.** We'll find the technology that has the depth and scope to provide the richness of service that you need. We'll bring this service to you through marketing channels that are convenient and easy to find and use. We'll enhance this product with others that make perfect sense to you, to create the context that is a logical extension of this product, from your point of view.

Of course, customers won't know all this unless you tell them. How far along you are in your partnership before you announce it to the world is a judgment call.

Announce that you are first

Customers won't know you are first unless you tell them.

"I was here first. It's mine."

Getting the word out early is important because you are not just talking to your potential and current customers.

You are also communicating to your competitors: we have seized this piece of ground. We are planting our flag. This section of beachfront is occupied and we are taking over this chunk of customer territory. Of course, competitors may also be jostling into the beachfront. They may be making announcements about entering the same space, too.

Whether you get to the beachfront first, or with others in a rush at about the same time, you can crowd out your competitors by lining up alliances and partnerships to expand your footprint on the beach. These aren't empty handshake deals—you must then mine those relationships for access to mutual customers.

But as you do, you're in a position of strength as the company that is first, or one of the first, to recognize the importance of this market and to dig deep to serve it. That impresses people—potential partners—who also want to reach the same market, and together, you can make much more noise about your intentions and get customers' attention much faster than if you were on the beachfront beating your drum all by yourself.

Competitors are unlikely to be intimidated, but when you are first or among the first, **they are forced into the position of not just putting their own ideas and approaches out there, but reacting to your strategy.** They have to recognize you in some way. If you have locked up some exclusive partnerships, clearly your competitors will have to find (second-rate) alternatives. Even if you have partnerships that are not exclusive, you were smart enough to get the best terms for your deal—the most prominent logo placement for your industry category or the sweetest revenue-sharing deal. Your competitors must choose to follow what you are doing—which tacitly forces them to admit that you are the leader—or they must choose a totally different tactic. And because you've figured out the best, most direct route to the target customers, your competitors are forced into a detour, or maybe an off-road strategy, like spending millions of dollars more to gain awareness to compensate for the avenues of marketing and recognition that you have locked up.

Some companies announce before they've hung up the phone on the conference call that sealed the terms of the agreement.

Others wait until the thing is completely sealed and the product or service created and fine-tuned before they let that press release out.

I've always made sure we announced Starbelly partnerships as soon as possible.

Not only does it create awareness in the

market, which generates inquiries and starts
to fuel the success of the partnership, but the
publicity also helps find beta testers—the first
one or two customers who are eager for the
service and are willing to help us refine the
execution.

Be the first to redefine an existing market

Biz Dev can help your company turn a
service into a niche market, if you make the
first move. Think of a cookout—but your grill
breaks. Where can you get the replacement
part you need?

In 1995, Brian O'Donnell, owner of a
small hardware store, realized that he could take
advantage of the Internet to meet his customers'
constant requests for replacement parts for
their Weber grills.

He cut a deal with Weber-Stephens:
O'Donnell's store would relieve Weber of the
headache of answering customers' questions
about grill parts and fulfilling their orders for
little parts, if he could retain ownership of
www.webergrill.com—the domain name that
O'Donnell had already registered for his store.

Weber executives were happy to cooperate. O'Donnell ended up shifting two employees to the grill site and struck similar deals
with manufacturers of camping supplies and
imported baby strollers. O'Donnell didn't
create the demand for replacement parts, but
by collaborating with the manufacturers and
moving swiftly to corner the markets he wanted,
he sweeps in nearly all the business that comes
to the manufacturers through the Internet.

O'Donnell didn't let himself be boxed in by the relatively mature demand for household goods like grills and camping equipment. By relieving the manufacturers of the hassles of dealing directly with consumers, he created a new niche for his store—one that now accounts for over 5 percent of sales revenue.

Reset the parameters through Biz Dev

Dozens of Web sites devoted to serving small businesses cropped up in the late 90s, all with similar missions—to amass an array of services critical for small businesses, offer volume discounts, and provide an online 'collaboration' space.

Most of these sites aim to line up the related products—shipping, printing, travel, computer retailers, auction sites—so a small business can find them all in one place.

Biz Dev creates credibility—it displays your effort to create value.

But which site do you think has more credibility: Ideacafe.com, founded in 1995, which has no discernible partners or marketing alliances; or Onvia.com, founded in 1996, with marketing partners that originally included AOL, Bloomberg.com, and *Business Week*, and that picked up Visa and trade association partners such as the American Business Women's Association, the American Management Association, National Small Business United, and the American Subcontractors Association?

Which site seems to be reaching deep into its market and grabbing credibility by pulling others onto its bandwagon?

Which one do you think gets a broader perspective on what its target customers want—the one that doesn't appear to have any partnerships, or the one that has tentacles into a dozen trade groups that each represent tens of thousands of small business owners?

Right: Onvia.

If you have read the market correctly and integrated specialized, hard-to-find services as well as more commonly available ones, each partner's credibility and market status is enhanced by inclusion in the group.

Logical aggregation of services to meet the needs of a very specialized market is an extremely appealing way to gain control of a niche.

Other companies trying to serve the same market are then forced either to scramble to line up their own menu of services, or somehow come up with a rationale for not doing so at all.

Either way, they are reacting to the market leader's re-definition of the market.

Biz Dev Buzz: Being first forces the competition to react, to catch up.

Measure your speed

Biz Dev means putting speed in your cross hairs, thinking about it, focusing on it, working to develop it. How do you measure speed?

- **Absolute speed:** How fast your company is compared to a neutral baseline, moving from idea to deal, and from deal to launch.

- **Competitive speed:** How much noise your company makes about its speed, through mutual press releases, interviews, ads, and other channels.

- **Real speed:** How fast and how well you leverage your partnerships to deliver the products and services that you promised your customers in those press releases.

"Horses and falcons not withstanding, it was only in the machine age that people became aware of speed as a quality that could be measured, computed, and adjusted."
—James Gleick, *Faster*

- **Relative speed**: How fast Biz Dev, legal, tech, marketing and production staff move to convert announcements into actual products and services in collaboration with partners and allies—compared to how fast everyone could create those products and services before.

If you want to find out how fast your competition is moving, search news databases, industry magazines and your competitors' Web sites to see how long it takes from their announcement of partnerships and alliances to their execution and sales of those new products or services.

Treat Biz Dev as a process, not a project.

Overlay your own company's negotiation-to-delivery time frame. Where are you faster, slower, and neck-in-neck with your competition?

If you benchmark your own company's speed, relative to the competition, you can figure out how—and where—to get faster.

What internal processes slow down your competitive speed? If you move quickly through negotiation and execution, but hold back announcements of impending products until they are imminent, why? Do you think that your customers are assuming that you soon will be announcing these services, and so will check with you before they buy a competing product? Or is news of products in development leaking out through sales, marketing, and customer service, effectively undermining your intended secrecy as those staffers try to clue in customers that there is something great for them waiting in the wings?

You may be fast, but you can be faster.

Chart every step in the process of bringing in new partners and delivering new products that result from those collaborations.

Push every department and every person to do it better, faster. Revisit every touchpoint in your internal Biz Dev process chart at least every six months to see what new friction points have emerged so you can smooth them out.

. Look for bottlenecks. Then remove them.

Every company has bottlenecks and friction along the path from the point where a potential partner calls your Biz Dev staff to the point where the product is actually sold.

Biz Dev Buzz: Benchmarking lets you identify and eliminate the drag.

Check it out

To see some of the advantages of being first, look at eCredit, at **http://www.ecredit.com/ partners/list.html**

Thanks to the partners of EqualFooting, you can buy supplies, get a loan, schedule shipping even if you are a small business. See **http://www.equalfooting.com**

Even an Org needs partners, as you can see at the Forum for Women Entrepreneurs, at **http://www.fwe.org**

"Our experience of time changes with our moods, with our age, with our level of busyness, with the complexity of our culture."
—James Gleick, *Faster*

To see what a complex site GE Aircraft Engines built in a few months, see **http:// www.geae.com**

Now that Hewlett Packard gets it, you can see their Internet presence at **http:// www.hp.com**

Content, yes, and plenty of links, but not many partners, in the Idea Cafe, at **http:// www.ideacafe.com**

To see the way partnerships can get you onto thousands of other sites, browse through the MapQuest Web site, at **http://www.mapquest.com**

NextJet tells you how to become a partner, right on its site, at **http://www.nextjet.com**

Partners help distinguish Onvia, a small-business service site, from the competition. See **http://www.onvia.com**

Look at all the business resources that partners bring to Purchase Pro, at **http://www.purchasepro.com**

Maps, yes; partners, no: Rand McNally solos on the Web at **http://www.randmcnally.com**

To see how a small business built a niche on the Web, look for replacement parts at **http://www.webergrill.com**

Yahoo does so much Biz Dev they tell you how to sign up, at **http://docs.yahoo.com/info/business/**

Take Biz Dev to the next level!

For other resources, ongoing conversation, and the BizDev3.0 newsletter, join us at **http://www.BizDev3.com.**

Step 4: Customers connect the dots

Every company insists that it exists only to make its customers' lives easier.

But, particularly on the Internet, expectations outstrip the ability of any one company to meet them—never mind exceed them.

No company can be everything to all its customers all the time. But if you draw in partners, your company becomes a three-dimensional resource for the customer.

If you can't solve a particular problem, chances are good that a partner can. Even if you pass that piece of business along without a revenue-sharing agreement, you will still benefit in the relationship economy because you reinforce your customer's perception of you as an advocate.

Biz Dev lets you **anticipate** your customers' needs and serve them—profitably.

The problem with serving customers in the Internet age is that it's impossible to keep up with what they want and need. Every day—every hour!—market conditions change.

What you sold them last week may already be **obsolete.**

What you sold them last month has **definitely** become obsolete.

If you sell a complicated product or service that requires lots of detailed specifications, you know how frustrating it is to keep revising the specs and targets and strategies to reflect current market realities—because those market realities don't stand still for a second. The whole point of Biz Dev is to get the customers what they want, **just as they realize they want it.**

Let customers tell you what Biz Dev you should do

If you listen carefully enough, your customers are already nudging you to your next Biz Dev deal.

One customer of ours kept asking us to speed up deliveries on last-minute orders. The most time-consuming part of the process was having to ship the product to the decorator, who had to unpack, decorate, and then re-package it, causing extensive delays.

We infused technology into the supply chain to make it more efficient, allowing the blank products to be coordinated with decoration services, and decoration services to be moved to the facility where the blank products were stored. This resulted in superfast turnarounds on these very short lead times.

We could only have met that demand through Biz Dev, through partners who really worked with us—not just conventional suppliers.

Many customers of an online gift store are procrastinators, who want the store to work fast, to make up for their own slowness—but they are willing to pay a premium for that service.

The store is based in New York, but from talking with customers and reading their e-mail messages, the boss had a hunch that if he could somehow engineer same-day delivery around the country, he could deepen the loyalty of these last-minute shoppers.

He found an upper-end chain of gift stores that was willing to partner with him by carrying a preselected array of gifts for same-

The old goal was to bind customers to you by covering every request they could conceivably make.

But even companies like Hewlett Packard, that used to have scads of divisions covering every market from every angle, are busy spinning off divisions, and subdivisions.

Each of these spin-offs has real focus, and doesn't have to keep going to committees to get approval for a new project.

day delivery. Orders for same-day delivery that come by 1 PM are processed immediately and forwarded to the these brick-and-mortar branches. There, they're wrapped, labeled and sent on their way via local messenger services, arriving at recipients' offices by 5:30 PM. By partnering with a company that he might otherwise consider a competitor, the gift-store owner found a way to expand both companies' markets by offering kick-butt customer service.

Customers remember your company when you go out of your way to reach them like that. (It's in their best interest, after all!) They come back to you the next time they need to buy gifts or shirts. And because repeat customers are the most profitable customers, using Biz Dev as a tool to cultivate loyalty with your customers can translate directly into higher revenues and greater profits.

Caution: If a consumer's only contact with you has been virtual, the only human face the consumer sees is the delivery person. If your distribution channel partner hires surly staff, drags its feet, or fails to deliver on time, your customers will figure you don't care, or worse, you, too, are rude. Your delivery partner embodies your service.

In fact, developing a great fulfillment system can give you a way to Biz Dev dozens of new partnerships.

Case Study: Fultonstreet.com

Stratis Morfogen founded Fultonstreet.com in 1998 to sell one of the least forgiving products on the Web: fresh and frozen seafood.

"Your goal is to find out what makes it hard for customers to do business with you and then to eliminate each of these barriers as you redesign your customer-facing business processes. Remember, you may find that the barriers aren't within your business."
—Patricia Seybold, *Customers.com*

So when he started the company, he put a lot of energy into building first-rate fulfillment and customer service.

Partnering with software developer Accesspoint Corp., he created a customer software interface that he dubbed Gino the Maitre'd.

Gino is Morfogen's online alter ego: he remembers every customer's name and collects them in a database. Gino also directs and tracks the flow of inventory in and out of Fultonstreet's freezers and coolers. Gino even has a customer service rep call each customer's house to confirm that the delivery arrived safe and sound.

Fultonstreet's first season was so successful that Morfogen won awards for his customer service. It dawned on him that the system he had created could be leveraged to expand Fultonstreet far beyond his original expectations.

He started cruising the Internet looking for compatible retail sites that looked as if they could benefit from offering cooked lobster dinners for two (and that were unlikely to start up seafood operations of their own).

His first partnership was with 1-800-FLOWERS. Morfogen simply e-mailed Flowers' CEO, Jim McCann, and pointed out that the site didn't offer lobsters. Wouldn't lobster dinners complement Flowers' product offerings, and wouldn't McCann love to connect with Fultonstreet to do that? To Morfogen's astonishment, McCann agreed. "The power of e-mail is incredible," says Morfogen. "In the past, they wouldn't have given me the time of day."

Lots of other companies are giving him the time of day—seventy so far.

Morfogen now keeps three staffers busy full time trawling the Internet for likely partners, sending out introductory e-mails and following up. His pitch is direct: "We're Fultonstreet.com. We're a brand that you can trust. Don't listen to us, listen to (customer-care diva) Patricia Seybold (a vocal Fultonstreet fan)."

Stratis Morfogen tosses fish at FultonStreet.com.

"We'd like to get into a revenue-sharing partnership with you."

In mid-2000, Morfogen signed on with JCPenney to become its online gourmet food partner. He also forged a partnership as Amazon.com's gourmet partner.

By now, Morfogen has realized that his most marketable asset is not his ability to pick out the best salmon or to pack great lobster ravioli dinners, and send them half way across the continent. It's **detecting brilliant partnerships**. He's leveraging his reputation for

Don't be shy. Other companies are looking for complements to their products and services, too.

Biz Dev to raise $40 million in venture capital to acquire a same-day fresh-food delivery firm that operates in thirty-three cities across the country. His aim is to forge local alliances to create an online grocery for gourmet and prepared food, delivering restaurant-quality food to customers daily.

Jack Welch turned his old manufacturing company, General Electric, into a model of an Internet-enabled company within a few years. He called in his managers and said something like, "We better beat ourselves. I'm starting to smell these upstarts. Rather than wait for them to take us apart, I'd rather demolish ourselves. In six months, I want you to write a business plan showing how the Internet will beat us. Then remake your groups to get out in front." As the changes took effect, GE's customers began calling and saying, "Could you do the same thing for us?"

At first GE reacted like a traditional company, figuring their processes and tools were proprietary, local, unique.

Then they got it. They decided to provide software like their own and similar services to their customers, just because people asked for it. GE Capital Information Technology Solutions now lets GE partner in new ways with companies that used to be simple purchasers or vendors.

You serve your customers when you refer them to a partner

At Starbelly, our customers are businesses that want to stamp their brand on something tangible—a hat, a shirt, a bag. Nestle, for instance, wants that kind of logo merchandise for its employees, and to give away as part of promotions and marketing.

And because our core business is brands, we can also advise customers on managing their brands as a resource. We help them distribute and regulate the use of their logos, around the world. When our customers think of their logos, we want them to think of us.

Our graphic artists work with customers to make sure the company graphics look great when they're translated into embroidery or silk screen on items you can wear, touch, or give away.

Sometimes our customers ask if we can help them put their logos on stationery, brochures, or Web sites. Or they want to paint the logos on their trucks, or put them up on billboards, or turn them into neon signs. Could our staff help translate their logos for those purposes? Sure. Will we? Not on my dime.

But because our mission is to help our customers with anything to do with identity programs, we refer them to a technology partner for graphics that go beyond our scope. It's up to our partners to convert that sales lead into a paying customer, but we have already served our customers by saving them some time, and pointing to an expert, so they can get the problem solved.

Biz Dev Buzz: Surround your customers with services that reflect well on your company, and you increase your credibility with your customers.

Online marketplaces and vertical portals will be among the very first to create partnership chains that mirror customers' supply chains and buying processes. To thrive amidst the cutthroat competition in their niches, the vertical marketplaces must draw in ancillary products and services that anticipate tangential needs that customers have to complete services—such as packaging, invoicing and checking credit.

Source: Forrester Research, Inc.

Customers want the product faster than you think

When a company stores gas or oil in tanks around the state, it needs to know how much is left, to plan supplies and deliveries.

Until recently, a sub-contractor would send a field-service guy out to each tank, to drop in a dip stick, and find out. Once a month a report came in to the owner by fax.

Imagine what these field service workers must feel like when they discover they have lost out to the Internet. They probably never thought that their customers would desert them, to get up-to-the-minute information electronically.

How'd it happen? Look to Optimum Logistics, a company whose main focus is on collecting and analyzing supply data. Kenneth Bloom, Chief Operating Officer, says, "Classic businesses have spent years creating relationships with other businesses in their industries. Relationships were vested deep within each department in the organization in a very logical place. But now, with the Internet, new relationships are being formed."

One of Optimum's partners retrofits liquid storage tanks with computerized equipment that gauges how much volume is left in them. That info is wirelessly transmitted to a local radio controller, which is connected to the Internet.

Subscribers to the service now can find out how much oil or gas is in any tank at any time, instead of waiting for the monthly fax. The field service companies are being left behind in the dust.

"Companies that think their customers will stick with them out of habit will soon learn otherwise. Even large companies that seem to be well positioned and impervious to change will have to face up to the realities of competing in the digital age. The alternative is to be protectionist of their markets. Good luck!"
—Geoffrey Bock, Patricia Seybold Group

And Optimum's position with its oil and gas customers is strengthened because they find out what they need to know much faster than ever, and that translates to sharper ordering, and more on-time deliveries to their own customers.

Customers want you to develop partners—or else

Geoffrey Bock, a senior consultant with the consulting firm The Patricia Seybold Group, says **most companies do not recognize that Biz Dev is a customer-relationship tool.**

Biz Dev helps you serve customers in ways they never imagined—but always wanted.

Bock points out that as customers increasingly use electronic means to feed back to their suppliers what's working and what's not, **companies will start to run out of ways they can hide their weaknesses** and gloss over their unwillingness to compensate for those weaknesses through partnerships.

Customers will tolerate that for a short while if they trust the supplier, but it won't be long before their self-interest takes over and they realize they must find suppliers and vendors that care more about their customers' well-being than their own status quo.

Only when customers start defecting will many companies start developing alliances and partnerships in earnest.

Companies might find it easier to warm up to that change when they discover one highly motivating element of an open-door Biz Dev policy—**revenue sharing.**

When you've created a ring of partners and affiliates around your company, you've cut through vast amounts of market clutter for your customers. You gain status as an expert, too.

Figure out the companies that can provide measurable value to your customers, providing services or products that you can't, or won't.

Negotiate deals with those companies to make sure that they return the favor by passing back to you a percentage of the revenue they net as a direct result of your referral.

With this kind of arrangement, you strengthen your ties with that partner in a way that an old-fashioned pass-through referral never could. And you keep your current customers from straying.

I can just hear some of you thinking right now: "Referrals. Old game. What's in it for me?"

Wake up! **When you've created a ring of partners and affiliates around your company, you've cut through vast amounts of market clutter for your customers.**

"Collaboration with your partners, as well as market responses by competitors, can create a halo effect around your partnership rings."
—*Network to Net Worth*, Credit Suisse First Boston Corporation

Your internal process of choosing those partners and alliances means you can authoritatively explain to customers why they're likely to get satisfaction with those suppliers. You gain status as an expert. And you get some revenue you wouldn't have seen before.

Just as important, the ring around your company means that you are free to stay focused on your core purpose. You don't have to worry about whether or not you should add in this little function or that one. Here's one time when you can say without a sliver of irony, "That's not my job!"

This is good news for customers: they don't get a half- baked effort when some genius in your company decides to expand into an area he knows nothing about, and in which he has no competence, contacts or experience.

Customers will force you to spin off or partner up

If you really get so many requests for that related service or product, yet there's no compelling reason to add it to your core lineup, then you have two Biz Dev choices.

You can start up a company to serve that related, but separate, need and spin it off into your circle of partnerships.

Or you can cut a revenue-sharing deal with another company that does very well what your customers need to be done.

Of course, you do the same for the companies in your ring. You're in *their* ring, and that means that you relieve them of the temptation to get all fuzzy about what they're good at and what they bring to customers. Each of you helps the other concentrate on his own essentials.

PeopleSupport provides Web-based, real-time, real-people customer support for retail and business to business sites. VP of Biz Dev Brad Duea says that many of his clients are caught by surprise by a tidal wave of customers. Those with traditional methods of developing customer support typically assume that they'll be able to grow their internal call centers and customer support teams rapidly enough to handle any influx of business.

They're wrong, which is why Duea has a company to run. "Business development sneaks up on them," he says. "They can develop expertise in customer support, in twelve months and for $12 million. In twelve days, I can cut a deal with that partner to get them that expertise quicker."

Customer support delayed translates directly into customers frustrated, and customers frustrated are customers denied. PeopleSupport's corporate partners are suddenly faced with competitors popping up everywhere and often they have only a ring of technology partners to help them respond. By bringing a company like PeopleSupport on board quickly, the partners stay a step ahead of their competitors and capture the moment with their customers by giving them the individual attention they need, when they need it.

PeopleSupport concentrates on what it does best—taking care of customers who are in the midst of a transaction and need help to complete it. PeopleSupport's clients get to focus on other elements of their operations that are more central, such as making sure that the technological infrastructure is upgraded and that there's enough inventory to send out to those customers who are getting the online help.

The PeopleSupport site boasts about clients and partners.

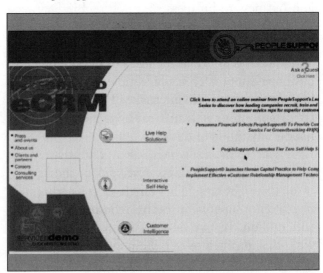

Both companies do what they do best, and by doing so, serve the customers best.

If you're really focused 100 percent on what your customers need now and what they're going to need in six months, you won't make them wait. You'll pull in all the resources that you can find to get that product to them today.

Make partnerships visible to your customers

Some companies base their business strategies on making their partnerships visible to the final customer, with the expectation that **the upward spiral of visibility will create perpetuate growth all by itself.**

This approach is working beautifully for iSyndicate Inc., which distributes content from almost a thousand original sources to almost 300,000 Web sites and in the process is making its corporate name synonymous with Web syndication.

iSyndicate could stay in the background— the delivery of the content wouldn't change a bit if it did.

But iSyndicate emphasizes that it's a partner with each content provider, so the consumer associates iSyndicate with more than 4000 reliable sources of information.

The clients want to provide an extra bit of value to their customers and iSyndicate just points out that it's the service bringing that content the last few clicks.

That visibility is a convenient and powerful marketing tool.

"The race is on for travel Web sites to align themselves with partners who will help them survive the category shakeout predicted by major e-commerce research firms. Bear Stearns predicts that only 20 percent of the estimated 1,000 current travel Web sites will survive— and those that do will have either aligned with the airlines or figured out how to fill niches too big for the airlines to care about. "

—eMarketer

*The iSyndicate Web site invites visitors
to search all its feeds.*

Think of a recent product introduction
or re-launch.

- Which customer-service functions
  were handled well in-house?

- Which ones could have been handled
  better by bringing in a partner to
  zip the product through distribution
  channels more convenient for customers, or to provide better customer
  support during or after the transaction?

- Which partnerships should be made
  more visible, for your company's
  sake?

Biz Dev Buzz: You're known by the
company you keep. Introduce your partners
on your site and in your materials graciously
and thoroughly.

Check it out

If you like fish without ice and sawdust underfoot, look at the way FultonStreet has expanded with partnerships, at **http://www.fultonstreet.com**

To see some of the products and services GE has spun off from its own Web infrastructure, visit the engine site at **http://www.gecits.ge.com/**

For a glimpse of a content provider making its partnerships visible, see **http://www.isyndicate.com**

To see the range of partners Optimum Logistics has signed up, look at **http://www.optimumlogistics.com/partnerships.html**

To see customer care for the Internet, with a good list of partners, at **http://www.peoplesupport.com**

For a wonderful introduction to customer-centric thinking, see the site for the Patricia Seybold Group at **http://www.psgroup.com**

Take Biz Dev to the next level!
For other resources, ongoing conversation, and the BizDev3.0 newsletter, join us at **http://www.BizDev3.com**

Step 5: Negotiate without baggage

Where does negotiation fit into Biz Dev? It is Biz Dev.

Biz Dev is negotiation. They are the same thing; they're synonymous.

No one can be good in Biz Dev without being a good negotiator. You won't get off the phone, you won't get anything done in Biz Dev, if you are the kind of person who walks in terrified to try to get a car for $300 less than the guy is asking—you aren't going to get anywhere.

But in Biz Dev we negotiate without a lot of baggage. There is no template, there is no one to tell you how to do it. You just do it, and learn how, and eventually you get good at it, or quit.

Imagine going to buy a house and applying for a mortgage, only to find out there is no standard mortgage form to use. You need to sit down with the bank and negotiate **every** term in the entire mortgage. What's your starting point for the negotiation with the bank? Nothing more than your perception of what your relationship with the bank should be, along with a fundamental understanding of the economic reality of your position vis-à-vis the bank.

Sound scary, a bit daunting? Well, what it sounds like is the essence of Biz Dev—the creative construction of innovative relationships through a new flavor of negotiation. Negotiation without baggage.

You negotiate already

Of course, you are already negotiating all day every day, whether you call it that or not. You are negotiating with your spouse about where to have dinner. You are negotiating where to go on vacation. Life is a series of negotiations. Of course, I usually lose the negotiations about where to go for dinner.

In any kind of Biz Dev negotiation, you begin with a fundamental idea about how the two parties can work together to make money. "Let's start a joint venture." Or "We're going to buy you." Or whatever. You start with the initial spark—a meeting at a trade show, an idea inspired by a magazine article you read, an exploratory phone call—and you articulate your vision. You bounce the vision off the other party. And you hope that you have two parties who fundamentally agree, "Oh, this thing would be great if we could do it together." At some point, almost instantaneously, the fluff is over, and you begin negotiating. Sure, sometimes there is a little lead generation, or creativity at the very beginning, when people are just, really, brainstorming, but that goes pretty quick, and after that you start negotiating.

In developing Starbelly, we had Biz Dev going trying to get new clients, new partnerships, new relationships, new suppliers, new channel partners—and new employees. Almost every new employee we brought on board came in through negotiation. We would find someone who had talents and could add something in the technology area, so we would enter into some kind of negotiation trying to get him to come on board. We had to negotiate pretty quickly because we had people who were fast paced and had lots of opportunities. Good sales, marketing and operations people—they were in demand. And at that time we really just had an idea, a vision. There wasn't much here. Some people came to us, in a natural extension of relationships we already had, but of the 230 people we added, we had to negotiate with most, and we had a very short amount of time to convince them that they should leave their jobs, or move. That was negotiation, like when we would call a synergistic company and say, "Let's do some kind of strategic alliance."

Fundamentally, to negotiate well, you have to figure out ahead of time what you are trying to get out of the deal. You have to sketch out a clear road map of where you want to go. And you have to assume that the other person also has a pretty clear picture of what he or she is trying to get out of it.

It's a process of give and take, so there's going to be a lot of selling, trying to convince you that what I am offering is really going to work out in the long term, or is really beneficial to you, or I have to do it because of this reason or that reason, and you're telling me what you need, and why the deal has to be different. And if we are going to reach a deal, we have to traverse those paths to get to common ground.

> "Affairs are easier of entrance than exit, and it is but common prudence to see our way out before we venture in."
> —Aesop

Homework?

I took a negotiation class in law school from a professor named J.J. White, one of the leading experts in business law. He has written books on negotiations for lawyers.

Law itself is just a series of negotiations. White's basic premise was that the guy who does more homework, who researches more, who knows the law more, is going to win the negotiations. So, knowing that, a good friend began the class by telling him, "I will read nothing, I will not research anything, I will not do one minute of homework, and I will only take the class under those terms." He got an A.

He would sit down with people who had done all the homework, and knew all the cases, and they would say things like, "In *Johnson v. Johnson* they said this, that or the other thing," but he won the negotiations.

That's why I say that you have to know where you want to get, right off, and very often that comes from gut instinct. You may not have a super-clear picture, though. Sometimes you just have a feeling like, "If I hire all these people and pay them all this money, I am going to be in big trouble, so I'd better use these brackets." Or "We want to cut this deal with Yahoo! but here is how much money we have in our budget." And sometimes you do not know in financial terms exactly what the Net Present Value or the Return on Investment is going to be.

Biz Dev negotiating is not as simple as buying a piece of machinery, where this is the output, and that is how much I will pay. Those terms are clear.

Sometimes you just have to hope that where you are trying to get to is the right path. You have a rough idea of where you want to get to and with that you begin the process of barter and bargaining.

Just close your eyes and jump in

Negotiating is not a esoteric talent that you're born with, like hand-eye coordination, which endless practice can only improve so much. Negotiation is something we can all master—the more you negotiate, the better you become.

There's nothing to be afraid of. It's like riding a bicycle, or playing tennis or golf. But you have to do it a lot, because some negotiations you win and some you lose, and only over time do you learn. You begin to be able to read people. You realize that when you took this approach a month ago, it really annoyed this guy, and he ran out of the room. You get more comfortable in the zone of negotiating. In fact, you get much better the more often you do it.

Basic negotiation is going to buy a car or a house. Most people have some experience doing that. You go in, and the guy says "I can only sell at the sticker price." Or he runs over and sees the sales manager and runs back and says, "I got you $200 off."

And you're negotiating. It's a process where you have to hang tough. Obviously buying a car is different from negotiating with a supplier, where they are going to bring a lot more to the table than you are, and you really want to get that deal done. Your leverage starts in different places, and it is going up and down all the time. I go to buy a car, and I am pretty confident that I can get a car at a good price, because I can walk out and go see another dealer down the street.

Negotiation is fundamentally a process. You could walk into a thousand different car dealerships, and negotiate differently each time.

"Man is an animal that makes bargains. No other animal does this—one dog does not change a bone with another."
—Adam Smith

There is no right path or wrong path. There is no "Follow these ten steps and you'll be a great negotiator." It's a relational process, two people talking back and forth, and you can see where you get stuck, if you're paying attention, and you're listening and observing where things are not going well.

People are generally pretty open.

They will usually come out and tell you where they are coming from or what they have to have, and you can also read where maybe they have puffed it, like where the salesman comes back and says "I can get you $200 off," and you say, "Well, I went to the dealer down the block, and he said he would give me $500 off, so I think I will go give my business to him." You get up and start to walk out, and the salesman comes running after you, "Wait! Wait!" and he goes to see his guy again. So there certainly is a lot of back and forth, and that's the process.

So don't be afraid of negotiating. You just have to do it a lot, and pay attention, and be willing to compromise. You have to have some idea of where you're going, and what you want to get, and what you can and can't give up. Sometimes you know what landmines you have to avoid, too. So you go back and forth and hope that by the end of the day you are going to get a deal.

Speed means a few bumps

Very often with a tech start-up you are crazed, because your Biz Dev life cycle is so tight you are trying to get something done in a week that normally would take other companies six months or a year to do, and you realize at the end of the process that you have missed something, or you were wrong about a detail. I can't begin to tell you the number of times I end a negotiation and realize, oops, I didn't think of this, and I proceed to address that one point.

One time we were negotiating with a company that wanted to be a strategic partner, and one of the elements of this fifty-point deal was us allowing them to use our technology, and they would relicense it.

Well, the way this thing was worded, it was like a conversation where I say one thing and you hear another, so they had thought that we would let them relicense our technology for free, in an unlimited capacity, but we thought we were going to give them that right in a very specific niche. In the fifty-point deal, the wording was very limited and very finite, so we had to go back several times to try to refine that point.

That's an example of a landmine—a thing you have to avoid. You can sit down with a company, and they say "We are willing to invest one million bucks," and if their guy says, "But you got to put up five million bucks," that's a landmine. There's no point in proceeding. You know where your company can and can't go.

The big difference between Internet negotiations and old world negotiations is the speed at which these negotiations take place. Other negotiations do not consider speed as a key function. Folks talk about getting the deal, but no one talks about compressing the cycle so that it becomes a different process altogether.

Speed is a key element of Biz Dev negotiation.

Mistakes are good—just open your eyes, learn from them, and keep going.

"Fortune and love favor the bold."
—Ovid

The Biz Dev negotiation cycle takes place at Internet speed. You're negotiating on the fly, and that's why you may have to come back and revisit an issue you missed on the first go-round.

Now, in a big established company you're going to have to sit down with four different groups of people over a week or so, and figure out the impact, before the next negotiating round. So you don't make many mistakes, except dragging your feet.

In a technology start-up you have two days. You want to get it done by Friday to announce it the following Tuesday. So your propensity for bad deals is much higher. You have to live with that.

Biz Dev Buzz: In the E-conomy you are turning deals more quickly and turning more of them—so the percentage of bad deals is much higher.

I'm blue, you're yellow—Let's find the green together

Biz Dev negotiating isn't like a Pepsi product development meeting, where you sit around for a week thinking about how colorful and bright you can make your bottle. This is raw business.

This is not creativity, where I am going to come up with a new ad campaign that is revolutionary. Business development has the word *business* in there for a reason. People have different interests but hope to find a way to align them. Think of the great partnerships or alignments. Imagine Ford and General Motors sitting down to form their auto exchange, Covisint. They have very distinct positions. Ford wants one thing, and GM wants something different, and they are both huge companies with very specific directions, and mission statements, and here they are sitting down and saying, in this one area, our interests may be more aligned than competitive. So how do we find a way to get it done?

You are constantly going back and forth until you find common ground. And especially with these very large players, you are starting with very different playing fields.

A lot of the great Biz Dev is done between a company that is doing something very specific and another company that is doing something totally different, and somehow there is a commonality between the two. For instance, I make credit cards, and you have a bunch of gas stations, so we can go make gas station credit cards.

"Business is a combination of war and sport."
—André Maurois

When we go into a negotiation, we take a very green approach to it. There is nothing personal about it. We don't care how big our name is, or how big the sign is, or the kudos. All we care about is the money. That's a wonderful attribute in negotiations, because not everybody is motivated by profit, with money as the driving force. Some people are motivated inappropriately, counter to the profit-making of most businesses. When you are in business, you are in business to make money—you may have shareholders, who want dividends and returns, and profits.

And often we are negotiating with someone who is motivated by something else—especially in big companies. If you have someone in the lower ranks of a big company negotiating against you, and his major objective is not profit generation, he may be worried about how good he is going to look, and how it will work out for his team. But fundamentally, all good companies reward revenue and profit generation.

Corporate games and back-stabbing only take you so far. Yeah, sure, in some companies, they take you all the way.

But in good companies, profit is what counts. If you stay focused on the bottom line, and concede all the yak that doesn't have to do with money, you can give up a bunch of stuff that has no effect, and still clinch the deal—and the cash.

What we negotiate about

In any kind of negotiations, there can be billions of permutations. It's not like buying a car where you have, well, delivery date, and price, and financing, and whether there is a full tank of gas—very few components that can be negotiated. In Biz Dev there could be millions of variables. You have only a hazy idea what will be important to the other team, or not important. But even though there are infinite permutations on the deal, there are only a few very large variables. You want something, and they want something. You want to make money, they want to make money. Profit is a variable, then—and risk. The extent that you can live with risk is a variable.

Negotiation often boils down to minimizing risk for both sides.

If I looked at a hundred negotiations and looked at what issues they have in common, I would say we were arguing about how we divide up the money, and who generally would bear the risk and the expense. Those issues are common to all negotiations. You can sense that the other guy is concerned about:

- How much money is he going to make?
- How much risk is he going to take on?
- How many resources is he going to have to devote to this?
- Do you have the resources?
- How will we divide up the terrain down the road?

> "All business proceeds on beliefs, or judgments of probabilities, and not on certainties."
> —Charles W. Eliot

The future is the biggest unknown: I don't know where I am going to be, so I wonder: How is this deal going to carve up paths I might want to go down in the future? Especially in Internet negotiations, you argue about where their core business might go, and nobody really knows, so they want to narrow the scope of this new venture.

The personality of negotiators

In Biz Dev, as in sales, there are personalities that are more conducive to cutting deals. You have to read that. You can send somebody in, and you see they clash with the other team's lead negotiatior—you have two personalities that are like oil and water. So clear the air by removing your guy.

My point is, in the new world your objective is to cut deals quickly that are going to be meaningful to your company and advance it, so you have to take all the things that traditionally

held up negotiations in the old economy, and get
them out of the way. For example, if I have two
personalities that don't mesh, and one company
says, "That's our chief negotiator, and that's the
end of it," well, we send somebody else in.

Or lawyers—lawyers kill deals. If you are
going to be negotiating these deals, you need
to be familiar with the law, enough so you
understand what can and can't be done. The
objective is to get the lawyers out of the equation
until the very end, and keep them on a very
tight leash, because lawyers have an extremely
finite perspective, which is to **reduce risk and
exposure. That is what they get paid to do.**
They are not paid to make miracles happen;
they are not marketers. They are paid to reduce
the liability of their clients. So in bigger deals,
they can kill or sidetrack a deal, make it take
four months instead of four days. But if you
have sophisticated parties on both sides of the
table, who are comfortable enough with the law
so they know where they can and cannot go,
you get through much quicker.

The 1, 2, 3s of negotiation

Here are the fundamentals of negotiating,
the basics to keep in mind.

1. Look for the stress point

In an intense negotiation there is very
often a stress point at which the deal could
fall apart. This is a wonderful moment in
negotiation. When you're buying a car, and you
walk out, and the guy lets you go, you know
$1,000 off is where he lets you walk out the

door. So if you get $800, you know, I am
in great shape. But $1,000—I have pushed
him too far.

When I am uncomfortable in a negotiation, because I have a roadmap of where I want
to go, but some permutation is sidetracking
me, I try to push as far as I can, to see at what
point I have pushed it too far, so that I know
I can't go any farther. Being aware of the other
person's feelings gives me that signal.

The last challenger on *Survivor* was asked
to name the kids of this person who was kicked
off the island—he couldn't name one. He didn't
know one personal fact about the people he had
just spent forty-two days with. But when they
asked him why he won, he said, "Because I was
attentive." Somebody said to him, "Attentive?
You failed the quiz." He said, "I wasn't attentive
to how many kids you have, I was attentive to
what you were thinking and where you were
going and what kind of personality you were. I
was tactically playing the game all the time and
I was observing all the time."

So I would say negotiating is not so much
about psychology, the personal aspect, but
about what is motivating this person, what he
will do, what he won't do, what is pushing his
buttons, what is making him uncomfortable,
where he is willing to bend. And how can I
get to a place where I am comfortable, given
what I am observing?

2. Be willing to share facts

When I negotiate, I tend to tell people
exactly the truth, exactly what is going on. A lot
of people in negotiations try to hold back what is

going on, and won't tell you that much. If I were a car dealer trying to sell cars, I would say, "Here is my cost for the car, here is exactly what I am paying, I want to make a thousand bucks, I am willing to make 700. That's it." Sometimes I am going to convince you to give me an extra hundred bucks, and sometimes not, but I am going to get more deals done, and sell more cars by telling you, "Here is my invoice for the car. This is what GM is charging me. It is only fair for me to make some money. So pay me the 300 bucks, and here's your car and it's clean and it's got gas, and I'll be here when you call me." That is our style. We'll go in and say this is exactly where we are. These are all the facts on our end. This is what we can do and this is what we can't do. Our approach is very rational. We have to rely on the partner being rational, and, you know, we get a lot of deals done.

A lot of time is saved in this way. You don't have to spend weeks finding this stuff out. Hey, in the end, it is all going to be exposed anyway.

These Biz Dev deals are broader, more intrusive, much more like real partnerships than they were in the past, so at the end of the day you have to figure that if you are going to have a long-standing good relationship with this company, they are going to know whatever you didn't tell them, anyway. If you were lying to them, it will come out. So our approach is to lay it on the line.

3. Keep the goal in mind

The key thing to keep in mind is that the points you gain and concede must add

> "If information is symmetric, trust substitutes for control."
> —Philip Evans and Thomas Wurster, *Blown to Bits*

up to deliver the end result that you want for the Biz Dev relationship. You need to be able to analyze the future impact of what you're agreeing to.

The bigger the deal—in terms of money that's changing hands, the degree of intimacy among the partners, and the potential impact on the company's revenue—the more likely it is that negotiations will get hung up on one of the two dozen or so main points. That is simply because there are so many main points. Concede points that aren't important to you—like which company's name will lead off the press release announcing the partnership.

Have in mind numerous tactics for getting what you want. The more imaginative you can be on the spot, the greater the chance that you'll be able to find common ground with the other party.

Bring to the table:

- **A firm grasp of what you want.** Make sure you have buy-in from key executives at your company before negotiations lay your company's motivations and priorities bare. Executives need to have an analysis by a Biz Dev staffer who is not involved in the deal attached to the paperwork when it lands on their desks for review so that they understand the context of the deal, the goals for the alliance and what options were thrown off the table.

- **A detailed understanding of what motivates your potential partner—** where it is moving in the market and

"Form your own keiretsu. Look for some way to become a part of a network of companies that work together."
—Jonathan R. Aspatore, *Digital Rush*

what hot buttons your counterparts across the table are most likely to respond to—speed? depth of collaboration? revenue sharing? This will inevitably come out in the negotiations as you discover which items are truly nonnegotiable and which ones your counterpart doesn't seem to care about.

"You need to be realistic when approaching larger businesses and present them with a clear-cut plan that benefits both sides."
—Jonathan R. Aspatore, *Digital Rush*

- **Your own due diligence package** ready to go so you can equip your new partner to move the deal forward if you reach an agreement quickly. The importance of clean, tidy paperwork can't be overestimated. Not only does it speed deals along, but if you are a start-up, having the paper ready to go signals your professionalism.

- **A willingness to defer to the top execs,** who may have brokered the meeting to begin with. Let them shake hands and set the tone. Make sure you make it clear that you are handling the details after the doors are opened. Reinforce your point by coming up with reasonable projections of the various unhappy outcomes that might result if you did pursue a deal that you have dropped—just in case the company president does call.

- **The desire to get to know your counterparts** a bit socially—at least, enough to get a gut feel for their corporate culture, whether or not your companies are moving in sync to reach your mutual markets, and what attitude they are likely to bring to the follow-up phase of the deal. You may find yourself negotiating with another Biz Dev guru, or a purchasing agent, or a corporate lawyer. Find a way to become aligned with that person.

- **The courage to move into a frank, honest, all-cards-on-the-table discussion** of what you can do for each other. "We're here. You're there. Our customers are in that corner. Let's brainstorm about where we can excel together to serve those customers."

- **The determination to agree on the broad parameters of the deal.** Who will get what? Give what? What kind of compensation, if any, will change hands, and for what evidence of what performance? Keep your focus on the key elements of the agreement—those that will add up to generating revenues and profits.

According to Harbor Research Inc., these four factors are critical in a Biz Dev agreement:

- What should the **alliance's specific charter** be in terms of market or technology focus and development?

- **How will management control be configured?** How and by whom will key managers be chosen?

- **What indicators should be used** to evaluate the alliance's performance and individual objectives of the individual parties?

- What specific options should be established for **altering or abolishing** the alliance and how should assets be valued and distributed?

Don't bring to the table:

- **Key research and development projects** that envision completely new products, or major advances with existing products. These represent your company's future new markets and revenue streams. Don't discuss the fact that you can create products that customers don't know they want until they see them—until you are ready to cut deals involving distribution and marketing. The one exception: tech collaborations that help you compete on the Web to begin with.

- **People who think that playing devil's advocate helps your cause.** Your goal is to look for common ground, rather than reasons why you and your partner should **not** work together.

- **People who get hung up on details.** Your first meeting is about sketching out the broad parameters of the deal. Lawyers, accountants, and IT and marketing staffers can iron out the details according to the agreement you have already forged. Help them stay on track, focused on the fundamentals, and pull them back if they start to wander into a thicket of unnecessary details.

- **A take-it-or-leave-it attitude.** If it seems that there are fewer synergies than you had first thought, a freewheeling brainstorming session might result in even better ideas than you started with. If you're on the wrong end of a take-it-or-leave-it offer—and many start-ups find themselves in exactly that spot—realize that you probably won't be able to persuade the other person to relinquish his position of 'power.' You will, in fact, have to decide whether to accept or not.

Take Biz Dev to the next level!
For other resources, ongoing conversation, and the BizDev3.0 newsletter, join us at http://www.BizDev3.com

Step 6: Deliver more than the deal

Why bother going to a concert? You've heard the songs five thousand times. Why do you do it? Because you want the experience.

Delivering on a deal, making it come to fruition, is like soaking up the beat, the band, the explosions, the lights, the crowd. Signing the deal is just hearing the song. Delivering is going backstage.

You buy Nike, sure, because you need shoes, and maybe you saw a fantastic ad, or you saw a player wearing them, but for Nike, the most important thing is that you expect that next week or next month, you will see another great ad, and another great player showing off that logo. You take home the shoes. But subconsciously, you anticipate the future value.

A deal is an investment—worth the net present value of its full future promise, discounted back to today. To get that NPV, though, you have to prove out.

In this chapter:

A deal is not a deal until you both deliver

Make sure you can both do the job

Prepare to follow through, before you deal

Get everyone behind the deal

Go the extra mile for your partners

Delivering on your promises keeps growth going

Biz Dev Toolkit

A deal is not a deal until you both deliver

Some companies just make a deal, and forget it. They don't follow through.

Delivering means more than shipping out a dozen t-shirts, extra large. Delivering means following through, and following through, and following through, so that your partners learn they can really rely on you, and customers do, too.

"Many employees tell me that at their old companies, 'People promised things that they just didn't deliver.'"
—Yolanda Gonzalez, CenterBeam, quoted in *Fast Company*

Biz Dev means nothing if your company falls down on the job of delivering what it promised to its partners in the heat of negotiations. Your partners feel disappointed, your mutual customers get mad—and, in the end, you lose.

United Parcel Service is a company that works hard to deliver—to partners and consumers. Ross McCullough is UPS's Senior Director of E-Commerce, and he makes sure that the company's Electronic Commerce Account Managers go to new partners' offices and show how they can take advantage of UPS tracking and efficiency tools throughout their internal operations and customer support.

No UPS partner is abandoned at the threshold. Each has an e-commerce account manager. "There's a joint effort to be sure we're complementing our business processes," says McCullough.

UPS and the partner start by creating a baseline of the partner's average transaction cost before UPS steps in, and then, after the partnership has been fully operational for a while, measure that cost again.

Even if a partner pays more in actual shipping costs, the additional value that UPS adds to its logistics and shipping operations—pre-truck—results in a drop in the average cost per transaction from as much as $2.50 to as little as 9 cents.

The account manager smooths the way for an efficient mutual operation, from calling on the IT department to fix technological glitches to advising on packing techniques.

If the alliance isn't delivering results for the partner, it's not working for UPS, either.

Too often businesses lose energy once a deal is signed. The excitement fades, the attention wavers. It's as if a college star took a big signing bonus, then forgot to show up for training camp. **Biz Dev doesn't stop when you sign. Like a person, the company has to follow through.**

The specifics of your follow-through arrangements will vary by the type of partner and the type of deal.

It's up to the Biz Dev team to choreograph the amount, level and timing of collaboration to be sure that the partners receive what they bargained for—plus!

Technical partnerships require intimate, daily collaboration of the partner's tech team with yours, as well as your company's IT executives. Glitch-free performance of the technology infrastructure underlies many partnerships, even those with relatively low-tech operations. If the computers fail, you will not even be able to collect data on the overlying functions—if you can perform them. eBay was excoriated

Treat each partner as carefully as if it were your only one.

repeatedly in the summer of 1999 for not having sufficient computer back-up and contingency plans. When its computers collapsed under loads of extraordinary traffic, eBay officials had a public relations mess on their hands, with thousands of sellers, which in effect function as partners.

Marketing and distribution partnerships that involve daily maintenance depend on periodic huddles and daily updates among each partner's marketing, distribution, and strategic planning teams to be sure that the partnership is continuing to deliver the intended value to the market. If revenue sharing or any other sort of payout is part of the deal, the accounting department must be in the loop, too.

Marketing alliances require the least amount of production and maintenance. They may be as simple as the partners designating each other as 'preferred providers' and posting each other's links and logos on their respective Web sites. Even so, Biz Dev must track the effectiveness of these alliances so that they can be expanded if they are successful or disbanded if they are not.

Partnerships drive customer ssatisfaction, and the need to satisfy customers is what drives partnerships.

One company we worked with early had decided that they would only allow their customers to buy through the e-commerce framework they had set up with Ariba. Everything had to go through Ariba. We had to figure out how to work with Ariba for our customer's sake—that was part of what we had to do, to deliver. The effort showed our partner how much we were willing to do, to fulfill our promises and keep the alliance going. And the hard work turned out to help us in another way—now, we partner with Ariba.

As the market continually changes, following through means making sure that the spirit of the alliance comes to fruition, maybe even more so than the literal details. All along the way, continual communication with partners is critical so that you are dancing in step with them as they respond to their markets.

Biz Dev Buzz: As your company's Biz Dev guru, it's up to you to make sure that partners know that your whole company will move heaven and earth to deliver on your deal with them.

Make sure you can both do the job

Occupied with getting their Web sites up and looking pretty, companies in e-commerce habitually overlook the critical elements of making sure that they can handle the orders that subsequently come in the door.

That's the view of Steve Saltwick, vice president of marketing for ClearCommerce, Inc., which provides as-needed e-commerce and customer support for transactional sites.

If most of your Biz Dev efforts pivot around developing marketing channels and co-branding efforts, fulfillment may not worry you.

But the more deeply enmeshed your company is with its partners, the greater your risk if you or your partners falter in the delivery aspect. So Saltwick urges you to **make sure**

When you coordinate all the resources at your disposal to make sure that your partners get even more than they expected from your agreement, you continually strengthen your bargaining position with future partners.

that your company can do its part to be a good partner and fulfill its obligations—and vice versa.

TheStore, for instance, is a company that depends on partnerships. TheStore will set up a private-labeled online store for anyone. They hook up lots of other stores' products, bundle them into a single user interface, slap your logo on the user interface—and you have a store. TheStore's equity rests on the shoulders of its partners. Without partnerships, there is no company. TheStore makes money by organizing and making sure its partners are doing the job. That is the heart of the E-conomy. We look at partners as defining the core business, not just supporting or supplementing. If one partner does not deliver, everyone is hurt.

Saltwick points out that the partners who are looking out for your best interest are the ones to keep. "It's the payment processing partner who says, 'Hey, you're getting too many fraudulent credit cards' that really proves their worth," says Saltwick.

Prepare to follow through, before you deal

On the racetrack—or on the Web—speed only matters if you have traction. Without traction, you are just spinning out sand, mud, and smoke.

At first, follow-through was not central to Biz Dev, so companies spun their wheels, issuing press releases, talking about links, pretending to be partners; but nobody down in the factory did anything different, and the partnership didn't go anywhere. Nothing got

Partnering for its own sake, with no follow-through, sets a dangerous precedent suggesting that partnerships aren't to be taken seriously.

fulfilled. "Do deals" was the mantra, not "Get the job done."

But for Biz Dev to pay off, the culture has to get a grip on the road. Like auto testers, you must quantify how every rotation of the wheel leaves a mark. **The more footprints you make** the easier it is to define progress.

Remember the footprint on the sand on the moon—that proved something real had happened. If the astronauts had just floated around, they wouldn't have made such a deep impression.

To prove that your Biz Dev efforts are worthwhile, you have to make tracks, change your products, adjust your services, act on what you saw when you got the deal going in the first place.

Start-ups should build the idea of fulfilling the Biz Dev promise into their cultures even before they cut their first deals.

If you help employees get it about Biz Dev right from the beginning, you won't have to suffer through remedial training sessions about how your company treats partners and why it's so important to take your commitment to them seriously.

CapacityWeb, for instance, was just getting organized in 2000, but its top executives were already mapping out the way that they will become full-fledged, operational partners. The company's mission is to create an online marketplace for the exchange of manufacturing plant capacity, allowing companies that aren't running at full tilt to sublease their operations to companies that currently have too much work for their plants to handle.

When Amazon.com partnered up with Drugstore.com, Jeff Bezos, head of Amazon.com, described Peter Neupert, head of Drugstore.com, as great at asking questions and getting to the bottom of a problem. "He's a driller. Lather, rinse, repeat."

Our hero, Jack Welch of General Electric, teaches us to do a 360-degree performance evaluaton, to see how each person is working with peers and subordinates—not just their boss. Try that in Biz Dev. Look all around you—inside the company and out—to see how a deal is working out.

COO Scott Hazlett and Director of International Business Development Pablo Toledo both have operational experience with heavy manufacturing, and they know that CapacityWeb will not have a chance if all its partnerships aren't perfectly orchestrated.

Follow-through will begin when partners start getting a steady stream of customers for their idle plants, or locate a plant that can handle their emergency manufacturing when overflow orders come in. But additional partner services will be essential. Bureau Veritas will audit the quality of actual production of manufacturing plants and verify that a run was successfully completed to a CapacityWeb customer's specifications, even if the customer never actually sees it. Freightquote hopes to garner much of the shipping that emanates from the customer's jobs, and eCredit expects to finance some of it.

CapacityWeb's ideal partners not only know their slice of manufacturing, but also can think outside the plant to detect additional services that they could create with CapacityWeb and jointly market through the site, says Toledo. For instance, they hope to ramp up their global network of factories to be able to offer a rapid prototyping service and create a track for super-fast manufacture and introduction of brand-new products.

At each level, CapacityWeb will have to draw in more partners to provide the necessary support services. Its ambitions will ride to reality on the success of these first partnerships.

Case Study: ENVISIONeT

Heather Blease had no experience with business development before she started customer support outsourcing firm ENVISIONeT in 1995. Fortunately, she's a fast learner and determined to get along and succeed.

When she left her technical job to start her own company, Blease knew that she would need every scrap of expertise she could muster to raise capital, bring in her first customers, and develop marketing strategies. Her first run with Biz Dev was when she teamed up with a small group of complementary companies that joined together for the express purpose of marketing their pooled abilities to Fortune 500 companies. Blease used the contacts she developed there as a springboard to land her first national account: providing online and phone customer support for Internet service provider Prodigy, in 1997.

Since then, Blease has had her hands full expanding ENVISIONeT fast enough to handle all the business that her partnerships rope in. The company now provides phone and Internet customer support for a division of Microsoft and numerous other ISPs and Internet retailers.

From her initial experiences with Biz Dev, Blease knows that she stands her best chance of winning clients if her team has worked out all the details of exactly how ENVISIONeT and its partners will support the clients **before** opening the first meeting.

"It's easier for a client to work closely with a team that's prepackaged and determined to get along, with technologies that mesh, as

Look for ways to leverage every partnership experience that you have. Even those that fall apart can often yield valuable referrals.

opposed to an ad hoc group that was selected individually and then became a team by fiat," she says.

Increasingly, she is leveraging ENVISIO-NeT's ability to pull together the precise combination of partners' technical resources for each client as a marketing trump card. Two non-exclusive partnerships already regularly help ENVISIONeT handle European projects and are called in when a client needs fulfillment, distribution and back-end order processing services on a spot basis.

"**We'd never enter into an exclusive partnership because we'd never be able to take on business outside of it,**" says Blease.

"There are (competing) companies out there that provide end-to-end customer solutions, including what we do, but it's better for us to figure out a couple of good strategic partners to deliver the best-in-class services and fulfillment," she says.

"It just makes sense. Ultimately I can talk about the virtues of partnering with a straight face and honestly feel that, for my clients, it's the approach I'd choose."

Get everyone behind the deal

We've had our own headaches with this. One operating partnership we struck was supposed to be announced within days of the deal. The Starbelly Biz Dev team got all the critical information to the public relations firm that we were using at the time (but not anymore). And we waited to get the draft of the release. And we waited.

The agency just didn't get it.

To them, this was a routine announcement.

To our new partner, it was a chance to make a **major first move** into a market they considered vital.

A month went by, and we couldn't extract a release from our agency. Meanwhile, one of our competitors got hold of the partner, and used the delay in announcing as evidence against us. The competitor persuaded the partner that we wouldn't be able to deliver on any other aspects of the partnership if we couldn't even get a simple press release out the door.

A good point—and one that the partner bought. Our agreement fell apart, and our would-be partner linked up with our competitor. All for the lack of a simple announcement.

Everyone who touches the deal has to understand why it's so urgent. If they don't, you'll see deals fall apart due to unnecessary bottlenecks, delays and misunderstandings.

Make sure your suppliers and vendors have the vision, too.

Follow-through used to be simply called 'operations.' That was back in the days when each company was able to control the entire linear process of its customer fulfillment and satisfaction. If there were problems, chances were that they could be solved in-house—because they originated in-house.

But Biz Dev growth models distribute the responsibility for follow-through much more widely, inside the company and among its partners. The simplest problems arise from miscommunications among the Biz Dev team and the partners. Harder to sort out are

Urgency=success. The more urgency surrounding a deal, the more likely it will work.

"A lot of companies are just doing deals with other companies because it's the damn thing to do."
—Ralph Syzgenda, General Motors

problems that result when employees deep within a company don't understand why they need to co-operate with an outside partner, or when managers outside the Biz Dev department don't put Biz Dev partnerships high on their priority lists.

Case Study: FreeMarkets

"Change the rules before someone else does."
—Ralph Seferian, Oracle

FreeMarkets is a company that really does a great job harnessing the Internet to change the way procurement agents work. You can make a market out of anything you buy. If I buy $3 million in office supplies, I can set up an auction, to let everyone bid on those supplies. It's a new way to buy.

But using FreeMarkets only works if every part of your company helps you understand what you buy, and why, and when it's needed. Everyone has to get together to do that. FreeMarkets has transformed the way companies can buy stuff, and entire companies have changed the way they do business because of it—the way they put together requests for quotes, the way they buy.

"In just under 5 hours, the FreeMarkets process saved 4% for Owens Corning across 27 shipping lanes. For this online auction, FreeMarkets received 512 bids from 36 carriers, delivering over $500,000 to the bottom line."
—Ad for FreeMarkets

In the old days the agents would go through a thousand meetings with suppliers, barter back and forth, secretly, privately, dysfunctionally, taking a lot of time—very inefficient. People were trained to barter in fragments.

FreeMarkets forces them to understand how much they buy, who buys it, who uses it, quantifying that opportunity up front. With more analysis up front, and auctions, **the whole process is more efficient**—but every purchasing department has to go through a radical makeover, to take advantage of this market.

Go the extra mile for your partners

Our company services the world of music—we partner in lots of creative ways with tour promoters, bands, radio stations. One partner is KISS-FM, a Chicago radio station. One day we got a last-minute call for a load of KISS t-shirts. They wanted some bands to wear the shirts during a concert—that night. Because KISS-FM is our partner, we went out and got the shirts from a supplier, printed them, and handed them up to the band members while they were going through their final sound tests on the stage.

Another time, we were brought in to help a partner drive people to its Web site. They wanted to run a sweepstakes, with promotional items as prizes, capturing info about the visitors in a database. We knew promotional materials, but we did not have the sweepstakes discipline in-house. We had a short time line to deliver or get out of the way. This was not the time to bluff. So we reached out to another partner, a tech powerhouse who knew sweepstakes infrastructure, but knew nothing about promotional merchandising. Through Biz Dev, then, we made sure that the job was done to our client's specifications and satisfaction.

Biz Dev can be tough for both partners, with long stretches of **uncertainty**. But it's not as hard if you have partners who are also on your side.

Feed them bits of market intelligence, and they'll feed the same back to you. Fax them

Follow-through works because it lets the rest of the company fish through the hole that Biz Dev broke in the ice. This is where the deal is converted into reality.

"I have always admired the ability to bite off more than you can chew—and then chew it."
—William DeMille

articles that comment on a tough market they're trying to crack, and they'll send a choice referral your way.

Partner follow-through is the single most important test of their commitment to Biz Dev as a method of business growth. Compaq Computer, for instance, continually challenges itself to provide better service to its partners, and in mid-2000 introduced a services network that enables them to submit warranty claims electronically and do online troubleshooting of everything from technical to account problems. That's exactly the kind of service that communicates commitment to partners—and gets you leverage not only with current partners, but those you might ally with in the future.

While I've had my share of great experiences, I've recently discovered what I think is the greatest experience of all—spending time with my children. Every day I spend with my two daughters, Chloe (two years old) and Casey (one year old), I literally get to watch them learn something new, for the first time. Their amazement and enthusiasm for their newfound learning is nothing short of inspirational. Watching them learn, and seeing their joy, puts a smile on my face for the rest of the day. What's this got to do with Biz Dev?

Well, it sparks the questions, "Why do people lose that when they go to work? Why does being part of a particular department have to mean doing the same thing every day? Why can't businesses, like children, have that sense of wide-open eyes, that thirst for new experience?"

Biz Dev does have the power to **catalyze**

entire companies, pushing every department in the company to experience new things, and to expand beyond traditional boundaries. Good Biz Dev brings the opportunity for new experiences to every part of a company. And great Biz Dev does it as a discipline, not a one-off project. But it only works if the people within the company are open and prepared to work, the way Chloe and Casey are prepared to grow and learn.

Delivering on your promises keeps growth going

Partners sign on with the expectation that your company's services will only get better, and thereby boost their benefit, as well. Delivery as promised—or better—keeps the growth spiral going.

When your staff comes through for a partner, the partner's wisdom in linking up with your company is confirmed. Of course, the ultimate customer is satisfied, which reflects well on both companies. For employees in both companies, the importance of the relationship is underscored. That cycle leads to more problem-solving and more imaginative customer service. Pretty soon, your partner's customers are dropping compliments about how you helped them, and your partner is looking smarter and smarter for choosing you.

Case Study: BizRate

BizRate.com was founded in 1996 as a way for online buyers to rank their experiences with e-commerce retail sites. Part of BizRate's

"As you cooperate with partners, your mutual trust will grow to the point where you will be able to share databases, customer profiles and benchmarking. This will feed the partnership momentum as data mining yields insights that can result in additional partnering projects."
—*Network to Net Worth,* Credit Suisse, First Boston Corporation

business model depends on its ability to pull in revenues by partnering with portals and other sites with lots of consumer traffic, positioning BizRate's findings as both a consumer service and as evidence that the portal is concerned that its users have satisfactory shopping experiences. As the amount of information on BizRate increased, thanks to its feedback button on, by now, 4,600 stores, BizRate has been able to produce aggregate reports on consumers' online shopping habits. Market trend and prediction reports enhance the BizRate brand and consequently nudge up the credibility of its partners, too.

BizRate also found that its research enticed many consumers to check with it before they embarked on an actual shopping safari. So it started selling space on its site to merchants that its consumers deem reliable. Those consumers are five times more likely to buy something from participating merchants' sites than are random surfers. That's exactly the kind of results that BizRate merchant partners are looking for—a measurable reason to stay loyal to Biz Rate.

"Hierarchy is an organization with its face toward the CEO and its ass toward the customer."
—Kjell Nordstrom and Jonas Ridderstrale, *Funky Business*

When you create specific products and services as a result of a Biz Dev deal, you complete the link between idea and revenue. You are providing your marketing staff with a concept it can present to the market and salespeople with a specific product they can convert to revenues.

Success breeds success. As your company and partners work together to consummate the deal, they touch off an upward spiral of results, success, added credibility in the market, which breeds better deals, more results, added success

and so on. It's not unusual for this Biz Dev cycle to accelerate as it gets bigger so that even large companies are doubling their client bases in a matter of months or weeks. Just one example: in the quarter ended in March 2000, Oracle's total adjusted net income jumped by 80 percent and its sales of customer relationship management software rocketed ahead 179 percent from the year-before third quarter.

That puts even more pressure on Biz Dev to extend its relationships with partners to the point where corporate leadership might wonder if the function is critical enough to bring in-house—unless the function can be divided among several partners on a non-exclusive basis.

Biz Dev Toolkit: Effective Communication with Partners, Allies, and Customers

Who's responsible for getting stuff done? The people who can deliver on the promises in your deal are spread out through at least two different organizations, with different responsibilities and abilities. So you need to communicate smoothly, and swap data fast.

Start by organizing the Biz Dev follow-up teams around a matrix of communications accountability. Each external partner needs a single point person inside your company. The Biz Dev contact needs to work closely with the sales support staffer who handles the relationship with customers who are jointly being served by the partnership.

Successful Biz Dev teams make sure they don't miss any crucial connections between anyone in the communications triangle.

Set up:

- **Regular update meetings** among the partners and their sales teams—to detect problems early on and to make sure that all elements of the partnership are functioning routinely, as planned and per the contract;

- **Back-up contacts**—Who at the very least have access to the primary contact's notes and know who to contact to solve problems when the primary contact isn't available;

- **Periodic strategy meetings** between the partners—to ensure that their joint product is still the best option for their customers and markets, and to map out additional products and services that anticipate emerging market trends;

- **Regular measurement** of the quantitative results spelled out in the letter of agreement, be that revenue sharing, income, a certain amount of Internet traffic, or another specific result;

- **Adjustment** of the measurement if warranted;

- **Visits** by the partners to each other's companies and with other members of the Biz Dev teams to develop a deeper sense of the corporate cultures.

Managing the care and feeding of Biz Dev partners is a powerful platform for your own Biz Dev aspirations. You'll get to know your partner companies inside and out as you solve problems big and small, and your Rolodex of well-placed contacts will grow exponentially.

Check it out

To watch the deals rise, at the heart of the B2B kitchen, see Ariba's site, at **http:// www.ariba.com**

See how your site, or your favorite stores, are rated by BizRate, at **http://www.bizrate.com**

Need a factory with capacity to make your intake ducts, or aluminum castings? You might want to try CapacityWeb's supply chain exchange Web site at **http://www.capacityweb.com**

Look at the way ClearCommerce has put itself at the center of a web of partners at their Web site at **http://www. clearcommerce.com**

People and partners proliferate on this customer care specialist's site, at **http:// www.envisionet.com**

Pick a country, to get into the site, then look at all the partner news at FedEx, at **http://www.fedex.com**

To get details on the way an established B2B exchange works, check out the Free-Markets Insider newsletter at **http:// www.freemarkets.com**

Want to see the original snail mail organi-zation partner its way onto the Web? Visit the U.S. Post Office at **http://www.usps.gov**

Take Biz Dev to the next level!
For other resources, ongoing conversa-tion, and the BizDev3.0 newsletter, join us at **http://www.BizDev3.com**

Step 7: Grow it or kill it

The old definition of **loyalty**—stick-together-till-you-die—is dead. Long live the new definition—shared dedication to the customer, for the purpose of this project, product, service, or point of time in the market.

Partnerships must morph to meet your goals of satisfying your current and potential customers—and your partners. No relationship can coast. Each must be constantly re-evaluated with an eye towards cutting loose those that just aren't working anymore. Dissolving a partnership can be as important as forming it.

Biz Dev works only when all the parties involved are flexible—and sometimes, that means modifying a relationship to accomodate market realities and shifting market opportunities.

You may discover you are no longer able to keep your commitment to your customers with one partner, or get to market on time with another. One partner may turn out to be too rigid, another too lazy, a third may just lose interest in the market.

Biz Dev works only when all the parties involved are flexible—and sometimes, that means dissolving a perfectly satisfactory relationship simply because the market realities have shifted.

Look at America Online. Their business and partnership model has changed at least

In 1980, 2 percent of the annual revenue of the 1,000 largest U.S. companies was earned through alliances.
By 1996, that percentage had grown to 19 percent.
By 2002, it is projected to be 35 percent.
—John Harbinson, Peter Pekar, Jr., *Smart Alliances*

three times in the last three years. At first, their partnerships were deals (often cost free) designed to promote the use of AOL by association. By getting high-profile partners to endorse AOL as their official Internet partner, AOL figured they would be able to attract people to pay to use the AOL service. It worked. No more free partnerships.

Once the original partnerships led to tremendous consumer acceptance, AOL morphed their partnership model into one based on long-term financial commitments with their partners. These financial commitments took the form of cash payments, royalties, and revenue-sharing—a partnership of highest bidders. But the partners bid too high and these long-term deals were cut short.

America Online sprinkles its screen with links to many partners under its umbrella.

The model has now morphed into one
that looks more than ever like one in which
AOL acts as a partner. AOL is now attempting
to add value through partnerships in many
ventures that AOL believes could help sustain
the AOL service (wireless ventures, alternative
distribution points). Free doesn't work for AOL,
nor does highway robbery. They have begun
morphing into true partners.

Play the field

There are no templates or established
guidelines for **touch-and-go loyalty**, because
the market, the technology, and your customers'
expectations are constantly changing. You may
strike marketing deals with the same ally over
and over again, but each one will probably
be just a little different, the better to reach a
slightly different market niche. Maybe you're
sponsoring a slice of content on a Web site
geared for women in the hopes of reinforcing
your message to mothers, and then the site
decides to shift its emphasis to grandmothers.
**Partnerships in the Biz Dev model are
more like dates than monogamous marriages.**
Flirt with the boy next door when your car
needs a free tune-up. Go out on the town with
the rising young banker who still wears suits
to work. Party hearty on the beach with the
sorority girls. Ask the nerd who sits next to you
in poli sci and takes great notes to the formal
dance. As long as everyone knows that you're
playing the field, no one can complain.
**Think of old-style partnerships as
marriages.** Certainly, the companies taking the
vows called them that. These were marriages of

"Touch as many
nets as you can."
—Kevin Kelly,
*New Rules for the
New Economy*

convenience, with pre-nups and post-nups and nups in between. Everything was spelled out. Sometimes, they even had a reception (after the deal was signed).

Partnerships today aren't even serial dating—they're **playing the field**. As long as you're maintaining an open mind (not promising exclusivity or the impression of exclusivity), both you and your partners have permission to seek out additional relationships, even if they overlap. Many companies partner with both AOL and Yahoo, swapping money for preferred positions in search engines and commonly referenced sections of the sites. **You're only limiting the possibilities if you limit the field.**

Your only loyalty is to your customers

Yes, your only loyalty is to your customers—period. You're loyal to your current partners, too—as long as they are really serving your customers. To give your customers what they want, you may have to let go of your previous conception of partnerhips being exclusive, or all deals lasting for ten or twenty years. Agility in your partnerships will give you the ability to meet your customer needs.

Exclusivity is not a goal in and of itself. Sure, having an exclusive partnership might free both of you to work well together, especially if the partnership involves complicated, proprietary technology focused on a particular market. But you may have to let go of a partnership, or make it non-exclusive, if your customers need more services or products than

"Whoever is most impertinent has the best chance."
—Wolfgang Amadeus Mozart

the exclusive partnership can provide.

You can't expect that a routine alliance will sew up your category.

If you're selling flowers, chances are you cannot be the exclusive florist for your partner. That would limit your partner's revenue streams and his own relationship with his customers; he wants to offer them as many kinds of bouquets as possible and get a share of the revenue from each. That's why your partners probably want the freedom to create alliances with your competitors, or at the very least, other companies whose services overlap with yours.

Of course, you want the freedom to do the same in your market.

Also, there are **shades of exclusivity**. Your first partner gets your most intense loyalty, because that first relationship sets the tone for others, establishes a routine, shows your team how to work together. And the first important partner may turn out to be almost exclusive, without the contract.

Case Study: ELetter

One of the venture capitalists backing Eletter calls Howard Giles, its VP of Business Development and Sales, "an animal."

That just makes Giles laugh. He's persistent, he's perceptive, and he has gotten Eletter from zero to 100 miles an hour in barely a year. If that makes him an animal, then that's what he is.

Giles spent years as a sales manager for an air-conditioning manufacturing company before jumping to SurfWatch, an early Internet screening software company.

Longevity is just a byproduct. Longevity comes out of a relatively static market that doesn't demand many innovations, or from an unusually agile partnership in which both partners are constantly reading the market in parallel and choose—together—to adjust their approach to the changing market.

That's when he started to edge into Biz Dev. He divided his time between pursuing traditional sales for SurfWatch—selling licenses—and developing partnerships with nascent Internet content providers like WebTV. Even at the time, he was conscious, he says, of **the continuum** that starts with sales, passes through short-term alliances and ends in the realm of the traditional set-in-stone joint venture. "**As you move up the continuum, the relationships become more paramount than purely the revenue**," he says. "That's the difference, as you move from sales to business development. **It's the relationship and what that brings to your company**, though obviously there are relationships involved in sales, and revenue involved with business development."

When he landed at start-up Eletter in early 1999, Giles was firmly convinced that he wanted to launch it through Biz Dev. Eletter's technological framework enabling users to format a direct mailing piece, upload their address database, and send the whole thing off without licking a single envelope was in its final stages of development. Giles knew that he had only a few months to capitalize on the first wave of interest that would accompany Eletter's debut.

"It was clear early on that the small business service portals were amassing compelling services, and those weren't very difficult sales," he says. "Nobody else was doing what Eletter did at the time and it was a natural fit. It was sticky, so repeat customers would come (to the partners' sites) and invoke revenue stream."

In his first month, Giles landed HotOffice, iMall and Niku, but he was hardly satisfied. "You often start off slowly to get who you can get and build a portfolio of partners, but the real goal was a big player. That was the challenge," he said. "I had to break through to the big boys. That happened through the deal we did with OfficeDepot.com. I had a couple of meetings with them. They were in the process of bringing service solutions onto their site.

"But there was no sense of urgency. I had a meeting with a senior vice president of OfficeDepot.com, and he was interested, but said, 'We'll postpone this for about three months.' I had to get them to sign. So I thought fast and said, 'Gee, that's unfortunate, because I wanted you to be the first player in the office superstore space.' As it turned out, Staples.com had just announced in the stamps area, with NeoPost, and Office Depot had already had a relationship signed with Stamps.com, but hadn't moved forward (to make it public). I landed on that —that they didn't want to be beat to the punch by Staples again. I was able to leverage that angle competitively.

"That's one of your big drivers, **the first-to-market dynamic**. There are such low barriers to entry that the first launch really owns that move. We got OfficeDepot, and once we got them, we had instant legitimacy. The other tier-one players, they don't call you, but it (the first big partnership) allows you to go in there and overcome all that scrutiny. Start-ups are subject to scrutiny and once that starts, you lose the momentum of sales.

"When we went to Intuit (to propose that Eletter be on its small business portal), they said, 'Who else are you with?' They'd realize, oh, OfficeDepot, and they'd assume that all the due diligence was done. They asked a few cursory questions but they didn't want to see the production center and meet the vcs and see our financing papers. That stuff's a **rathole**. You can spend days bogged down in it.

"Once we got OfficeDepot, they fell like dominos….Intuit, Microsoft…You've got to get a marquee player, and the rest will come.

"Then that becomes a natural exclusive. OfficeDepot is the only office supply company we'll work with. They get a revenue share, typically about 10 percent of the cost of the service (to the customer), excluding postage. But frankly, they don't do it for the money. It's about adding value-added services to bring customers to their sites. The revenue share is peanuts—not that they don't take it."

Giles hardly considers his job done. He foresees a shakeout in the small business services market and expects that his Biz Dev agility will help position Eletter to avoid the worst of it. "The survival of the strongest depends on your ability to leverage channels and solutions, not by yourself, but through others," he says. "There's a tremendous opportunity to take what's out there and aggregate it in many ways, and build channels in different ways to leverage the strengths of many different companies and target markets that aren't being served now. **Business development will (partly) be the ability to leverage in a consolidating space, because everyone cannot get the profitability to survive.**"

According to consulting firm Booz Allen & Hamilton, American companies have entered into 25 percent more alliances every year since 1987.

Biz Dev Buzz: Nurture your relationship with your first major partner carefully. It sets the precedent for future partnerships.

It's OK to disagree

Don't kill a partnership just because of **hurt feelings**, or **misunderstandings**, though those can certainly undermine a partnership.

Even close partners will sometimes treat the relationship differently in private and public. They may not show the enthusiasm you feel, in their public relations, marketing, or Web site. If you expect your partners to publicize the relationship, you may be disappointed. You may find out that your new partner doesn't mind having its own logo splashed across your Web site, but prefers not to return the favor.

Is that a deal killer? Probably not, if the partner does its job, expanding your business, and serving your customers.

Case Study: Ariba

One of our partners, Ariba, makes Internet-based software that is taking over the world of corporate procurement. Their market acceptance has beaten even the most aggressive expectations. They know e-commerce inside and out. Not surprisingly, companies (like Starbelly) that want to ramp up quickly call Ariba first. Still, in early 2000, as e-commerce rubber met the real-world road, Ariba found itself short: customers were screaming for order-fulfillment and logistics software. Ariba had already helped them integrate their Web sites with their corporate accounting, inventory and operations. So of course customers called Ariba when their loading docks bottlenecked. "Just help us get the stuff out the door already!"

Ariba had to have an answer immediately. Instead of tossing the problem to its programmers, Ariba created an alliance, in spring 2000, with e-commerce firm Descartes. They make what Ariba needs: fulfillment and logistics software. Now, Descartes' software and logistics network—the people who know how to get a box of electronic widgets from point A to point B—is integrated with Ariba's commerce platform—the people at point A and point B who want to swap a box of electronic widgets for cash.

That's just a thumbnail example of the pivot-on-a-penny flexibility that has led Ariba to form dozens and dozens of first-class alliances and partnerships. Just among the traditional audit and management consulting firms, Ariba is holding hands with all the biggies: Ernst & Young, Deloitte Touche Tohmatsu, Grant Thornton, and both Andersens—Arthur and Consulting. That's because new clients often have strong existing relationships with their accounting firms—relationships that Ariba must work with if it is to get that business.

There's no gain to Ariba in choosing just one accounting firm as its only partner. None of them expects it.

In fact, the consulting firms don't seem to get it yet about how valuable their corporate partnerships and alliances are—not one of them highlights its existing partnerships on its home page, on its news pages, or on its e-commerce section pages. Instead, they carry on about new

The more desirable you are as a partner, the more power you have to dictate how other companies publicize and honor your partnership.

partners and papers and awards and branches just as they always have.

A partner like Ariba might be annoyed with this apparent cold shoulder, but Biz Dev isn't co-branding. Ariba builds **credibility** by making its alliances transparent to the buying public.

The accounting firms don't think they get anything by publicizing their ties to Ariba. Yet.

Flexibility cuts both ways

You can get left, or joined, at the altar. You have to figure that you may get jilted, and figure out how to adapt to a partner who drops you, slights you, or changes the relationship.

In February 2000, DuPont Corp. and Internet Capital Group said they would form a joint venture called CapSpan, to leverage ICG's experience in building B2B marketplaces and DuPont's "industry knowledge and strength as a large-volume buyer and supplier." That expertise would be applied to apparel, chemicals, construction, and e-procurement.

Great idea! Sounded as if ICG had scored a coup. Wow! DuPont! What a great deal for ICG's partner companies, which all focus on hard-core B2B functions. It was hard to imagine a better marketing alliance for ICG.

Unfortunately for ICG, DuPont decided to hedge its bets. Barely two months later, DuPont was publicly announcing its intentions to play the field. If ICG's partners fit DuPont's needs as it poured a billion dollars into its superportal, fine. But there was no

Small companies are getting in on Biz Dev: in June 2000, Arthur Andersen and National Small Business United released their annual survey of small business owners, and found that 21 percent say they'll engage in strategic alliances as a key business growth strategy. That's compared to those who are looking to acquisitions (14 percent), joint ventures (11 percent, and mergers (5 percent) as growth tools.

way DuPont was going to make any promises to ICG's partner companies. Suddenly, this deal started to look much less like a marketing-driven partnership and much more like a traditional client-consultant relationship, with ICG serving up its ability to build online marketplaces and DuPont flexing its global muscles to bring in its own premiere marketing partners. Of course, if ICG adjusts its perspective, it can make the most of its first-chosen status.

The freedom to change partners is inherent in the Biz Dev growth model. Once a company catches on to this, it will suddenly see possibilities in every direction and its historical pattern of forming affiliations will not slow down its rush to get in on the Biz Dev boom.

Expect contradictions

Misunderstandings may be inevitable when you are redefining what **loyalty** means. Some disagreements you can live with; others spell the end of the partnership. But loyalty does not mean sticking together no matter what.

Many companies, especially those outside the high-tech arena, may know that you aren't using the old definition of loyalty, but they aren't at all sure what you do mean by the term. You're not being mean-spirited, or Machiavallian, in being explicit about what you expect, as you're discussing terms of agreement. But even if you spell out terms carefully at the beginning, **you and your partner are both moving quickly, so you may well step on each other's toes occasionally.**

Mistakes are just part of the process—as long as you learn from them.

You may, for example, find yourself involved in a new business-to-business marketplace where your relationships are constantly shifting. Sometimes you're cooperating with a competitor in a reverse auction so you can both get a good price and immediate delivery on, say, a shipment of specialty steel that you both need. Other times, you'll be going against that competitor in a traditional way, and perhaps, in another marketplace—one that's owned and run by a handful of the leaders in an industry you both supply—you might want to cooperate with that same company to create a specialty product developed just for the needs of the companies that run that marketplace. None of these relationships counts as disloyalty. None forces a breakup.

The more fragmented your industry, the more likely you and your partners will take on many different, sometimes **conflicting, roles**. These partnerships get complicated, messy, self-contradictory. A reasonable outsider might look at the straight and dotted-line relationships you have with what used to be a traditional, stay-neatly-in-the-box competitor, and think that your company has no idea what it is doing. That's normal, in a Biz Dev world.

Usually, the reasons why you and a partner must go your separate ways aren't frivolous.

We've had to back away from some alliances as our business model has evolved—what was once a great deal suddenly didn't work well for either side. Rather than try to force the framework of the deal to fit the new reality, it's better off all around to recognize that the

> "Exploit flux instead of outlawing it."
> —Kevin Kelly, *New Rules for the New Economy*

> "As the Internet weakens the role of dealerships and resellers, many companies will be forced to figure out how to interact with their customers directly. In many cases, that means partnering with a wide variety of technological, distribution, and communication design consultants and service providers to create dynamic Web and offline touchpoints that constantly change, depending on market forces and customer use and expectations."
> Source: Morgan Stanley Dean Witter

value added for both of you has evaporated, and agree to let it die.

Biz Dev Buzz: If a partner's criss-crossing loyalties really undermine the relationship's value to you, cancel.

Pull the plug or swap it out

You'll know when a partnership or alliance just isn't working any more.

Pull the plug when—

- Your company's **strategy** has shifted dramatically and you're no longer serving the same customers as your partners.

- Your partner's strategy has shifted and they're no longer serving the same customers.

"I. Create!
II. Sell!
III. Implement!
IV. Exit!"
—Tom Peters

- The customers' **problem** has been miraculously solved by another product or service—or your customers don't care enough about it any more to pay to have it solved.

- You have a revenue-sharing agreement, but **no revenue** is being produced to be shared.

- Your partner's funding dries up and you fear that they won't be able to deliver their end of the bargain.

Renegotiate when—

- Your company's **strategy** has shifted dramatically and you're serving the same customers in a very different way.

- Your partner's strategy has shifted, too.
- A **new technology** appears, undermining your combined value to your customers.
- **Revenues** come in a different form, or for different reasons than you'd both anticipated.
- The Biz Dev staffers with the partner company seem **unable** to marshall the resources quickly enough or thoroughly enough to deliver value to the customers.

Let the market make you flexible

If you redefine loyalty to mean **devotion** to your customers, you're freed up to shift continually, to reflect, to lead your market.

You don't stay **attached** to your old ways of doing business, and, because you're not locked into any long-term relationships, you can learn from competitors' mistakes and quickly formulate strategies that outflank them, via Biz Dev.

When Ace Hardware decided (finally) that it had to go online, it didn't build an online toolbox from scratch like Sears, Roebuck and TruServ Corp. did. Instead, Ace got up to speed faster, and got some extra cachet in the bargain, by partnering with OurHouse.com, a home ownership and maintenance site, to provide its inventory and fulfillment.

Instant win-win: OurHouse now gets the advantage of the 5,100 neighborhood hardware stores that are members of the Ace cooperative, giving it bricks. Ace gets

Yahoo knows a thing or two about partnering, and it doesn't hit a home run every time. Though it signs a few new alliances and partnerships every week, it had to cut loose a high-profile joint venture announced in March 1998, with MCI, which was to provide a co-branded Internet service provider. The arrangement barely lasted five months.

the panache of the well-designed OurHouse site—not to mention the momentum that OurHouse has thanks to over 100 million dollars of venture investment.

Not incidentally, Ace gets to outflank Home Depot through OurHouse.com's **already functioning e-commerce operation.** At www.homedepot.com, you can fix it, build it, grow it, decorate it, or install it, but you can't buy it. You can only get directions to the nearest Home Depot store. Maybe that tab should be called Drive it. Ace could have shrugged off OurHouse.com as an upstart competitor—which, at first, it was—instead of learning from Sears' and TruServ's mistakes and trying to go it alone.

Your partners and allies also expect flexibility, so you can continue ongoing discussions with them about how market forces are changing your mutual customers' needs and if, and how, the partnership might continue.

You can take the most relevant, most useful parts of what your partners have to offer without being obligated to work with the entire operation.

Ace Hardware appears at the top of OurHouse. com.

Everyone wants the same thing: to cultivate loyalty among their own end users.

Your partners don't want to prevent you from achieving that any more than they will let you be a barrier between them and their own customers.

A lively, engaged partner who is constantly coming up with new, fresh ways to work together is a partner who is asked to renew contracts.

And you want your company to have the reputation of being astute and reasonable to deal with.

Don't stick with hopelessly obsolete contractual requirements; grant your partners favors when you can. Chances are you'll have to ask them for favors sooner or later.

Biz Dev Buzz: Constant evaluation of the market lets you drop or add partners, as you change the definition of your business.

Plunge into the chaos

When no one stays put, when every partner morphs as fast as you do, when customer dreams change every few weeks, you may feel you are in a sea of chaos. But instead of trying to back out (you really can't escape), plunge in.

Play with it. Experiment. **A culture of Try This has a greater chance of delivering interesting, profitable market adaptations that capitalize on these transitory market conditions.**

Vistify is developing software that will be added to specially equipped regular household appliances—like refrigerators—so

I am a big believer in immediate action, handling a piece of paper just once. Otherwise, I'd be buried. I'll fire off e-mails as I chat with someone, and by the end of the conversation, the problem is solved, or on the way to resolution.

That's one of the marvels of e-mail—shifting time and boosting productivity.

Without e-mail, my life would be a lot more chaotic. I also use a Blackberry to keep in touch around the clock. I send e-mail in the middle of the night, and get replies then, too. That wouldn't be possible with a telephone.

To manage the chaos, you need every available tool—computer scheduling software, cell phones, wireless e-mail, instant messaging.

that people can order groceries and household supplies whenever they think of it. Its goal is to simplify household e-commerce by aggregating information about routine purchases into a single touchpoint. Company co-founder Menekse Gencer says that she expects to have an ever-changing perception of where that device will be located in the house. It might start out on the refrigerator, be moved to a deck, and then live for awhile in the family room.

No matter where it is, Vistify's goal is to push special offers that are up-to-the-minute relevant. It's snowing? Vistify suggests that you add sidewalk de-icer and wool socks to your shopping cart.

"We are crazy. We should do something when people call it 'crazy.' If people say something is 'good' it means someone else is already doing it."
—Hajime Mitarai, Canon

"It's commerce at the point of thought," says Gencer. One firm criterion for her potential partners is that they should be able to track with Vistify's perception of what consumers want, now, and turn their production and fulfillment operations to accommodate that. In this changing environment, Vistify edges right up to chaos.

Sometimes, when we feel like we are wading into chaos, up to the hips, we complain that chaos is hard to live with, in and through. But Biz Dev folks who can learn to adapt and even **thrive on the edge** of chaos will reap the rewards when they push ahead, drawn by the goal of giving their customers what they want, when they want it, despite the hubbub.

"Skate to the edge of chaos."
—Kevin Kelly, *New Rules for the New Economy*

Chaos is **messy**.

We yearn to grow out of it—or just run away from it.

But in the middle of this energetic whirlwind

we can preserve our **enthusiasm** for finding new ways to do business and new ways to serve customers. We can even develop an acceptance of chattering, inconsistent, self-contradictory environments. Starbelly's growth was not quiet or peaceful. It was hectic, crazy, and disorganized. And it worked. Out of the chaos came a shared pursuit of a marketplace revolution, a pursuit shared by an entire company that was growing (at its peak) at a pace of ten people a week. We allied with every logical partner, and our minds were open to find the highest value of each partnership.

Biz Dev gurus thrive on this complex interactive system. They love the everything-up-in-the-air feeling of knowing that it all could change at any moment—the unnerving edge of chaos.

Not everyone can stand this **creative maelstrom**, but in a fast-growing economy like ours, everyone must develop a tolerance for it. Plans change. Some efforts are wasted. Partnerships fall apart through no fault of either side.

To be sure, this ill-defined, rapidly shifting world can be infuriating and frustrating. Partners come and go, unpredictably.

But for Biz Dev, bubbling chaos is also a sign of growth, even when you have to dissolve some outworn partnerships. Chaos just means more Biz Dev opportunities for you.

There is a common phrase in the real estate world, "Let the property be what it wants to be." Meaning that in order to maximize the value of a piece of real estate, the real estate developer needs to focus on the property, not

"You can't be a serious innovator unless you are willing and able to play. 'Serious play' is not an oxymoron; it is the essence of innovation."
—Michael Schrage, Tom Peters, *Serious Play*

See for Yourself:
If your company is already partnering with others, are there any arrangements that seem to be past their prime? Why? Can the relationship be renegotiated to reflect current market conditions, or would you recommend that it be abandoned? Why?

on his personal interests in the property. Biz Dev is much the same. Rather than focus on the people doing the deal, focus on the partnership itself, and figure out its highest value.

Partnerships are possible between **any** two companies. What makes those partnerships succeed or fail is the ability to find the **right** partnership for each situation.

Check it out

Not a member of America Online? No problem. Look at all the partners at **http://www.aol.com**

To see how Eletter leverages its partners, click the Partners option at **http://www.eletter.com**

Ariba's the partner behind the scenes at tons of ecommerce sites. To be amazed, click the Partners tab at **http://www.ariba.com**

For the partnership between DuPont and the Internet Capital Group, see **http://www.internetcapital.com/network/fastfacts/ff12.asp** or **http://www.dupont.com/corp/whats-new/releases/00/000218.html**

When Ace partnered with OurHouse.com, both won at **http://www.ourhouse.com**

Do your appliances need a partner? You might want to visit **http://www.vistify.com**

Take Biz Dev to the next level!
For other resources, ongoing conversation, and the BizDev3.0 newsletter, join us at
http://www.BizDev3.com

Step 8: Reach in to reach out

In Biz Dev, you have some partners you must communicate with every single day—your co-workers and employees.

How come they're so important?

It takes a company to support Biz Dev.

Just as no company is big enough to handle all the opportunities that a market offers, so no Biz Dev team can possibly manage all the preparations, negotiations, and follow-up necessary to keep business development rolling along with wow results.

When everyone in your company is a de facto member of the Biz Dev team, you can cut deals with confidence.

There are enough surprises for the Biz Dev team out in the real world. The greater the cooperation, enthusiasm, skills and personal resources you know you can assemble to enact a deal, the more imaginative and confident you can be in shaping deals.

You'll get great ideas for new Biz Dev, too. For instance, an artist on our staff, who is usually involved in putting graphics on T-shirts, was working on an image from classical art when he realized that there was probably a great opportunity to be had in brokering partnerships in the world of fine art, in order to access huge libraries of digital art. A month later, three partnerships spoke to the validity of his concept. A classic idea!

In this chapter:

Jump over traditional internal divisions

Biz Dev inspires

Biz Dev Toolkit: Organizing a Biz Dev Support Team

Case Study: Fed Ex

Starbuddies

Biz Dev Buzz: Evangelizing your own co-workers and employees is one of the best parts of the job.

Jump over traditional internal divisions

In doing Biz Dev you don't respect traditional joint venture and partnership rules. Ditto, internally: you have to jump across traditional divisions. One deal may require the close collaboration of two specialized IT staffers with someone from advertising and another person from customer service. The next day's deal might draw the Web master, an accountant, and two researchers into an ad hoc project group.

Values of an Also Ran:
• Minimize risk
• Respect the chain of command
• Support the boss
• Make budget
—Tom Peters

For most people, job descriptions and levels of authority have been all too clear cut. It's probably safe to assume that most employees, especially those with a decade's worth of experience, have had first-hand encounters with very structured company organizations that seem designed to prevent interaction across department lines and organizational-chart lines, not encourage it.

But **every person** in the company has something to offer your latest Biz Dev projects. A brilliant negotiating tactic might emerge from a debt collector. The guy in the repair shop might share his observation that a certain category of customer seems now to prefer sports cars over Cadillacs. If the opportunities you've Biz Dev'd are to propel the company's growth and profitability quickly, you'll need the ingenuity, imagination and dedication of everyone, not just a chosen few in Biz Dev, marketing or sales.

Biz Dev inspires

Top-down manifestos dictating changes in corporate culture do not always work. People want to be like the winners they know.

If you are trying to move your company from an old-economy mindset to an E-conomy mindset, showcase the exploits of the Biz Dev team. Other employees will be curious about this ongoing quest to open new frontiers. They'll be motivated to capture some of that fun and glory for themselves. Before you know it, much of the change you want to take place will be accomplished, without benefit of a single memo.

Be sure to connect the dots. Let people know about Biz Dev triumphs and disappointments so that the team's activities aren't a mystery to the rest of the staff.

To keep the **urgency** going, keep employees up-to-date on market conditions, the company's direction, and the Biz Dev team's aspirations, so they will understand why a hot deal is bumped to the top of an IT project team's list, or why someone in marketing has to clear his calendar to attend a Biz Dev deal-making session.

To engage folks who might not feel they are part of the Biz Dev effort, set up your own Starbelly sessions to encourage everyone to put in his bit.

Or set up a virtual or real bulletin board or other meeting place that's a no-criticism

Internal Biz Dev relationships parallel those outside the company. The Biz Dev team needs to explain its role and what the implications are for each department in the company. The same skills that open doors for the Biz Dev team outside the company will win them loyalty with co-workers.

zone where people can post their creative ideas. In these settings, you can overcome objections with sheer enthusiasm.

- **Biz Dev your own internal projects.** The way a Biz Dev team pulls the best of everyone's skills together to create a new partnership can also be the model for the way you assemble your internal follow-through teams. You draw more and more employees into the process—and they start to get it.

> "You are the storyteller of your own life, and you can create your own legend—or not."
> —Isabel Allende

- **Grow your own gurus.** Biz Dev isn't taught in any MBA program and doesn't show up (yet) in any textbooks. The only way you can add bench strength to your team is to pull promising candidates from other departments in your company and involve them in all aspects of Biz Dev.

- **Rejuvenate the Biz Dev team, to keep morale up.** Everyone wants to come home to a safe place where it's OK to be bummed about the Big One that got away. When everyone else knows what it's like out there on the sometimes cold frontier, they'll be able to provide support and solace when a guru needs it.

There is no greater team-building exercise than turning Biz Dev loose inside your company.

Example: Hans Peter Brondmo, chairman

and founder of Post Communications, an e-mail management company in San Francisco, gets his customer service employees involved in the Biz Dev process whenever they set up marketing and customer follow-up programs for new partners. His goal is for employees to get to know a customer's goals and technological setup so well that they can suggest additional services to the customer—and then turn around and collaborate with the partners to make those services happen.

The troops, unleashed, will surprise you with their enthusiasm to make their own mark on the frontier. Some will go there personally, others in spirit as they support the Biz Dev team. They'll all be together in the Biz Dev mindset, and your company will never be the same.

Biz Dev Toolkit: Organizing a Biz Dev Support Team

What a great assignment: working with the Biz Dev gurus to turn their deals into reality !

Here are the skills that the Biz Dev support teams need to keep the gurus working at full steam.

- **Administration**—You travel a lot, and when you're not traveling, you're holding meetings. You need an unflappable, organized administrative assistant who can make last-minute changes to travel and meeting plans, create PowerPoint slides, and make sure that all the guru's irons stay in the fire.

- **Research**—You need at least one crack researcher who can dig into SEC documents, industry associations and journals, search databases, and collect information off the street about wannabe partners to find out if *they* will be able to hold up their end of the bargain. This is a competitive intelligence job, for which there are a great number of resources available. Optional, but wonderful: an intuitive ability to pick up encouraging or discouraging signals about the potential ally's corporate culture and the tenor of its Biz Dev team.

> "Top-performing companies are two to four times more likely than the rest to pay what it takes to prevent losing their top performers."
> —Ed Michaels, *The War for Talent*

- **Project management**—As a deal comes closer to consummation, others representing the company's interest will get involved: lawyers, the CFO, the appropriate technical staffers, marketing and sales. Each needs to understand the scope and impact of the proposed deal so he can advise in turn, and prepare his own team for the after-deal follow-up. The project manager interprets the internal implications of the deal for everyone who will be part of the follow-up—and shepherds the follow-up process to be sure that everything the deal promised is delivered.

- **Partner Relationship Management**—Though this function overlaps with the project manager, the emphasis here is on constantly communicating with the partner's Biz Dev team to monitor its understanding of the changing market and the success of the deal as it plays out in the real world. The manager is charged with communicating the success or failure of the deal to the rest of the Biz Dev team and corporate executives. She will also be the one who knows how the execution of a deal might be adjusted to reap better results or reflect market demands more accurately.

- **Public Relations**—You've already negotiated whether or not to beat the drum, and if so, how loudly and in what direction, as part of the negotiations. Especially if announcement of the deal is intended to send a message to the potential market, competitors, and other partners, the public relations staffers need to be in the loop so they can prepare materials and arrange a press conference, if needed.

Case Study: Fed Ex

FedEx has done Biz Dev ever since it was Federal Express.

Well, sort of.

David Payton, now Director of Biz Dev and Alliances, has been with FedEx since 1979. "Even though it has become a catch-phrase for the new economy, we started a long time ago, working with partners in the early 80s. Our first one was Gelco, which helped us expand geographically into Canada. By operating with them it was a much faster road to expand into

Canada, than going through all the regulations and legal work to set up ground and long-haul operations in Canada.

"That was the initiator. We realized, hey, we **can** partner with companies. We don't have to build new companies. They were partnerships, but it was a glorified supplier relationship. It wasn't a meeting of equals, that's for sure."

In the mid-1980s, FedEx suddenly had competitors coming at it from all directions. Its partners were getting pitched by other companies and FedEx found itself trying to push into markets where it had much more formidable competition than it had in the United States. DHL, in particular, dominated the international quick-delivery category.

FedEx faced a clear choice: move away from a corporate culture, which was "almost military," according to Payton, with complete control over its 'partners' and everything that faced the customer, or cede markets to companies that were less rigid.

"It's hard for us to change our stripes, but we slowly but surely have afforded more trust in the (partnership) relationships, versus just us controlling it all," relates Payton.

The procedure that FedEx has settled on may seem cumbersome to some, but in reality, it represents a smart blend of due diligence and speed—and it is thoroughly consistent with the size of FedEx.

Dreadlocks and beer provided two early challenges to FedEx's growing trust of its partners. As it worked with local firms in foreign markets, some Latin American partners'

"Conformity is the enemy of freedom and the jailer of growth."
—John Fitzgerald Kennedy

employees had dreadlocks, which was "totally contrary to our personal appearance policy." And FedEx's 'fitness for duty' policy didn't square with the German custom of having beer with lunch.

"We realized that these folks (the regional partners) knew the cultures of the area better than we did, and we listened to them. In order to improve the quality of our service to customers, little by little, we started to build up a more trusting relationship with the partners."

In the late 1980s, FedEx started calling its technology vendors "partners," and restructured its contracts with them to share the cost savings netted from tech solutions they fashioned. That moved the relationships over the line from "vendor" to "peer," and made a world of difference, as the vendors capitalized on their empowerment by giving FedEx first crack at their latest, greatest ideas.

The quantum leap came when FedEx realized in the early 1990s that its slow rate of growth was being outstripped by upstart competitors who had a much more flexible notion of **cooperating** with partners. As that reality was dawning, the popularity of the Internet suddenly burst on the scene, offering FedEx a once-in-a-lifetime chance to completely reorient its philosophy of partnerships and distribution channels.

"We had customers coming to us in 1994 and saying, 'You guys are the leaders in technology. Wouldn't it be cool if we could sell our stuff through the Internet, and you could ship it for us from your warehouses?'" That inspired the Virtual Order service, which debuted in

1996. It created an interface for customers' inventory, shipping and tracking—and opened the door for the now-ubiquitous FedEx tracking service that's standard at many retailers and distributors selling through the Internet.

As the pace of technological change accelerated, FedEx realized that even with its army of 5,000 information technology staffers, there was no way it could continue to lead the shipping industry all on its own. In June 1997, Payton led the charge to officially effect a new FedEx policy that explicitly encouraged technological partnerships.

"It still wasn't easy," he says. Not only did internal IT developers feel threatened—both that they'd lose their jobs and that they'd get stuck with only brain-numbing internal maintenance projects— but many staffers also jumped to the conclusion that collaborating with partners somehow would be less work than developing software in-house.

"If you partner with someone, it requires an investment of time and resources. It's not free," emphasizes Payton.

"They thought, gosh, they've got the product and all we have to do is integrate it and, boom, we're done. But that's not the case. You still have to maintain the relationships and market the (value of the partnership). **If you ignore these partners, they'll find someone who is more attentive.**

"There's a lot of excitement in the beginning and the intentions are always the right ones. But because of the dynamic world we live in, new issues and challenges crop up, and as a result, the executive team starts focusing on (i.e., reacting to) new things that are hitting the radar (instead of focusing on pushing ahead with marketing initiatives). That's costly."

Payton's efforts to convert FedEx's internal culture have paid off. When, in 1998, FedEx reorganized into a holding company with divisions focused on different slices of the logistics and shipping pie, each of the new companies incorporated a transparent, open philosophy towards partnerships right from the beginning.

Biz Dev Buzz: Examine every idea that comes over the transom.

These days Payton's group catches and screens the constant gush of eager would-be partners—they come in at an annual rate of 600, sometimes as many as **ten each day**. Payton's Business Intelligence Group takes a serious look at every pitch, determining whether it's "a real company that's an operating concern or just a couple of guys in a garage with an idea."

Most potential partners are weeded out early on.

Some proposals are out of sync with FedEx's direction; others would dilute FedEx's core mission; and others are so flimsy that there's no 'there' there.

"I've had people send in ideas that practically say, 'Hey, I have an idea, pay me half a million dollars so I can buy a house,' and then you call them, and they have no technical qualifications or experience," says Payton. "I just send them a letter that says, 'Thanks but no thanks.'"

"Success is the ability to go from failure to failure without losing your enthusiasm."
—Winston Churchill

The group develops a thumbnail company profile that includes competitors of the would-be partner.

Many companies are eliminated at that point, but about half make it to the alliance review committee, whose members are drawn from the legal, finance, marketing, logistics and other departments. In their biweekly meetings, they examine the proposals for their consistency with FedEx's strategy.

If the pitch gets a green light, the business intelligence staff maps out possible structures that the deal might take. Their recommendations are taken back to the alliance committee, which, if it likes what it sees, creates an opportunity assessment team to formulate the deal.

"This is where we get all the (operating) areas really involved," says Payton.

"They don't want their agendas handed to them. We have found that out." The operational area that's most likely to work closely with the potential partner designates an executive sponsor who champions the proposal from there on.

"Leadership is a performance. You have to be conscious of your behavior, because everybody else is."
—Carly Fiorina, Hewlett-Packard

"I will not do anything if I don't get an executive sponsor," says Payton. "He has to come from whoever has the most skin in the game. That's how we're sure that they'll still be focusing on it in a year."

The team assembled by the sponsor digs deep into the potential partner, completing due diligence, examining its business plan, and coming up with an operating outline for the partnership.

Biz Dev Buzz: Let the person who has the most to lose by the failure of the partnership head it up. Because she has the most invested, she's likely to be the most motivated to pour energy and team resources into cultivating the relationship.

Proposals that survive the twelve-week-long internal obstacle course—and only 1 percent eventually result in partnerships—are sent to an officer review committee comprised of FedEx's top echelon.

The executive team from the wannabe partner makes a presentation to the review committee not just of what they do, but of what the mutual advantages of the relationship would be.

If it's thumbs-up all around (about 70 percent of the companies that get to this level are approved), the deal is sealed immediately and the new partner is shifted to a project management team that is responsible for executing the agreement.

The project manager is "**totally focused** on implementation," says Payton. The manager is also expected to cultivate such a close relationship with the partner that FedEx is presented with more ways that the two companies can work together and leverage the relationship.

Partnering with FedEx doesn't instantly preclude all other alliances with related companies.

"We don't offer exclusivity nor do we expect it," says Payton—but, on the other hand, FedEx does expect that the partner won't also partner with FedEx's direct competitors.

Payton says that the internal FedEx process enables it to garner the best of the market innovation as quickly as reasonably possible for a company of its size.

"In the past, technology was the differentiator or barrier to entry. Today, it's not. You come up with a technology and I promise you that next week, there will be a competing technology," he says.

"You have to choose your relationships carefully because they are your competitive edge. If you've done it right, it's unlikely that your competitor can match every feature."

The FedEx site lets their partners, and their customers, track orders.

Starbuddies

As Starbelly expanded, we realized that communication amongst the various departments of our company was likely to suffer, simply due to rapid growth. The larger we became, the more difficult it was to ensure that all of us were always on the same page. Lack of communication stifles the Biz Dev process, something we were not prepared to accept. Our solution was an innovative program called **Starbuddies.**

The program worked like this: Every single person in the company was part of a group of approximately six to eight other employees. The membership of the group was such that nearly every person in a Starbuddy team came from a different department, and they rarely knew each other at the beginning of the program.

After the Starbuddy teams were announced, the members went for a company-paid outing every two weeks or so. The outing itself was up to each team. Some simply had lunch every two weeks, some went to dinner, others went bowling or golfing. One group had so much fun together they even went to Jamaica (they paid for the trip themselves—Starbelly, though, bought dinner for them in Jamaica!).

The Biz Dev benefits were enormous. Although it wasn't required, conversation at these outings often turned to work issues, and by putting together, say, a group of people from accounting, programming, purchasing, sales, executive management, art, and marketing, amazing results were achieved. And these weren't all managers either—the majority were line folks who understood the day-to-day issues and had good suggestions on how to fix problems. Plus, now each employee had a "buddy" to call in another department, to answer questions and resolve issues, expanding the power of the program exponentially.

When you create a landscape ideal for Biz Dev, the entire company embraces partnerships and alliances, because everyone understands what the issues are, and why the partnerships will help your colleagues in other departments.

Check it out

Now part of Netcentives, Post Communication handles 75 million e-mails a month for some 40 million customers, at **http://www.postcomm.com**

Want to track your partners and their customers' packages? See **http://www.FedEx.com**

Fuld and Co. is one of the top competitive intelligence companies in the business. This is a collection of links they recommend for gathering CI over the Internet. **http://www.fuld.com/i3/index.html**

Stratfor is a kind of "private CIA" for corporations, and can deliver custom analysis on nearly any international topic. They also offer a wonderful free e-mail newsletter that focuses on the world's hotspots. **http://www.stratfor.com**

The Society for Competitive Intelligence Professionals site is useful for an overview of the competitive intelligence field. **http://www.scip.org/**

Competitive Intelligence: How to Gather, Analyze, and Use Information to Move Your Business to the Top by Larry Kahaner (1998, Touchstone Books). This is a great book for developing competitive intelligence techniques—nuts and bolts about how to elicit meaningful conversations from the competition.

Take Biz Dev to the next level! For other resources, ongoing conversation, and the sporadically published BizDev3.0 newsletter, join us at **http://www.BizDev3.com**

Step 9: Count the results

The one thing that everyone always asks about Biz Dev is, "How do you know if it's working?"

This is a reasonable question. Unlike a sales force, the Biz Dev team is not charged with responsibility for hitting certain revenue targets. Unlike marketing, our **impact** cannot be benchmarked through a statistically valid study and then checked again after a major awareness campaign. Unlike the IT department, we don't care whether data is being processed faster and more powerfully. Unlike the legal team, we don't want to point to lawsuits won, settled or averted. No such measurements will work for Biz Dev.

So, how do we know if it's working?

At Starbelly, we know that our Biz Dev team is totally rocking when we look at the number of deals in the pipeline. **Every deal represents a whole constellation of additional companies that we can come in contact with.**

Though Biz Dev is an indirect strategy for business growth, and its efforts overlay many other market-growing company efforts, we can track and quantify the results of our Biz Dev activity. We can prove we get results.

Define success

The way you define and measure Biz Dev success depends on what stage of growth your company is going through.

- **Pre-start-up**—Biz Dev efforts recruit the advisory board, help acquire seed financing, and begin to create an expectation of the company's mission that may attract talented executives and staffers.

- **Start-up**—Biz Dev cold-calls every logical potential partner to gain that first toehold of acceptance through lining up its first channel, distribution or marketing alliance. Meanwhile, the CEO and tech team settle on the technology partners that have the talent and resources to create the infrastructure required to launch the product.

- **Launch**—Biz Dev builds on its first round of partnerships by gunning for the big game: nationally known, tough-to-persuade partners who could dance with anyone. Bagging one of them is a coup and bolsters the company's reputation as it enters the critical launch phase. Biz Dev efforts help create awareness that may lead to early sales.

- **Growth Spiral**—Biz Dev now adds the critical component, making sure the products and services are delivered as specified in the deals. As the spiral funnels out, revenues start to

In traditional companies, every effort of every outward, market-facing employee is engineered to elicit a certain result. The unexpected still happens, but it is much easier to track the results of traditional marketing and sales efforts than it is to bottle and measure the effect of creating a Biz Dev aura around your company.

come in through sharing and other agreements. The Biz Dev team must continually feed the funnel to keep it ever higher and wider, creating a swath of cleared frontier for the marketing and sales teams.

Measure the market

Key measures of Biz Dev's impact on the market are:

- **Market share**—Biz Dev creates an atmosphere of awareness and expectation on the part of potential partners. Well chosen and executive partnerships will contribute to the company's market share.

- **Sales**—Actual paying customers who find your company because of your relationships demonstrate how Biz Dev efforts can drive directly through to the bottom line.

- **Revenue Sharing**—Income generated through affiliate marketing is relatively easy to track through partners.

- **Dotted-line impact on partners and allies**—They too should be growing, thanks to their relationships with your company.

- **Gaining credibility with investors**—This mindshare can eventually be quantified through the success of an IPO, the price of the company if acquired, or the amount of money the company raises through its next round of private financing.

See for Yourself: Where does Biz Dev have an indisputable, yet dotted-line, impact on your company's revenues and profits? How could you better quantify that impact?

- **Renewal of partnership agreements**—If your company delivers on its promises, many partners will work hard to find a way to continue to work with you.

- **Open doors for your sales staff**—Biz Dev efforts should make it easier for them to get in to large, lucrative customers and leave with completed sales.

- **Ease of winning new partners**—Your company's reputation for the care and feeding of Biz Dev relationships will have a big impact on your ability to gain credibility and commitment from new partners and allies quickly.

- **A reputation as a market leader**—Check out press and analyst evaluations and reports, the number and quality of invitations to speak at industry and business functions, and invitations recruiting your company's executives to participate in other companies' advisory boards.

- **New players lobbying to get in your doors** —One sign that you've arrived is that people you've never heard of now consider your company a prestigious and influential one to ally with.

- **Ability to move into true dynamic pricing**—The Biz Dev team collects and analyzes information from partners and customers in enough detail that you can figure out at any given moment what your product is

"All men's gains are the fruit of venturing."
—Herodotus

worth to a particular submarket—and you go out and get it.

Measuring Biz Dev may not be a formal effort. But if you take a step back with your key people and analyze your customer base, other opportunities you are pursuing, and the reasons why your customers think you're important, you will get a bird's eye view of the impact that Biz Dev has had on your status in the market. That's what Peter Russo, director of the Entrepreneurship program at Boston University, concludes.

"Biz Dev could very well be the difference between a 5 to 10 percent growth rate company and a 20 percent growth rate," he says. "And you may find that you have developed some real capabilities in serving your customers that can lead into opportunities to provide more complete solutions."

Keep track of your Biz Dev efforts so you can trace actual results to your ideas, contacts, introductions, deals and staff.

Even if you aren't quantifying every move that your Biz Dev team makes, you will be able to detect the positive repercussions of their influence. Review the year to see what they did that worked (and thus was expanded, with result) and what they tried that didn't work (and thus saved the company substantial time, effort and money by not heading into that frontier).

Face the failures, then. **The more deals you cut, the more likely that you will have a few stinkers.** That's especially likely if your company or your Biz Dev team is inexperienced with making lots of deals, quickly.

The disadvantage of speed is that it can limit the time a new team has to mull over the

"Throughout the 1990s, strategic alliances of the world's top 2,000 companies have produced an average annual return on investment of nearly 17 percent. That is an ROI 50 percent higher than these companies' non-alliance activities have produced."
—John Harbinson, Peter Pekar, Jr.
Smart Alliances

possible effects of a proposal that seems urgent. Oh well. Now you know.

Case Study: The Datek-Schwab shoot-out

Still not convinced? Here's a comparison of Datek's Biz Dev activity versus Schwab's, as provided in the top five press releases on their respective Web sites—with my comments.

June 7, 2000: **Datek Online Reports 89,104 Average Daily Trades for May 2000**—Yawn.

May 5, 2000: **Datek Online Reports 121,673 Average Daily Trades for April 2000**—Whoopee.

April 18, 2000: **Thomas Robards Named Chief Financial Officer of Datek**—The new CFO probably got a mention in the *Wall Street Journal*. Great.

March 9, 2000: **William Mohr Named Assistant General Counsel of Datek**—A lawyer gets his name in the *Wall Street Journal*.

February 22, 2000: **Datek Online Rebates $190,318 in Order Flow Payments**—They're giving some people money back.

Market commission rate: $9.95. Only one of the top ten online brokers is cheaper, according to Kiplinger.com.

Share of market: 10%.

Datek's entire output of press releases over a four-month span amounts to self congratulations.

By contrast, each Schwab press release—and note, by the way, that we're looking at a *two-week* span, not four months—is focused on **growing the business** in a different way, mostly through targeted Biz Dev.

June 8, 2000: **New Schwab Gift Package Makes It Easy To Give The Gift Of Investing to New Investors**—Neat way to bring new investors into the fold, certainly a Biz Dev strategy.

June 6, 2000: **Schwab Fuels Velocity Desktop Trading System for Active Investors With Streaming Quotes**—Schwab acquired CyBerCorp to make this happen; they didn't try to build it themselves. Pure Biz Dev.

June 5: 2000: **Schwab Launches Wireless Investing Service**—Schwab formed an alliance with Aether Systems to make this innovation happen. Pure Biz Dev. Cool technology too.

June 1, 2000: **Schwab and U.S. Trust Complete Merger**—A quote from the press release: "With the merger completed (we) can kick off development of a number of new product and service offerings that leverage each others' strengths." A Biz Dev play.

May 22, 2000: **Schwab Launches Life Event Series**—Service to help divorced and widowed folks get a handle on their finances. Nice. And it's Biz Dev.

Market commission rate: $29.95, the highest of the top ten online brokers, according to Kiplinger.com.

Share of market: 27%.

Where would you rather be? Slugging it out among the low-priced guys (albeit your Mom would see your name in the paper) or riding high with more market share than the number two and three competitors combined and the highest priced trades to boot? I'll take number one any day.

Case Study: W.W. Grainger

When Don Bielinski first started to get calls from cable and telephone companies way back in 1995, he wasn't sure what to make of them. The companies wanted to form strategic alliances using the Internet.

W.W. Grainger was a logical fit. The distributor of maintenance, repair and operating supplies (MRO) has over 1.5 million customers worldwide. They would sift through Grainger's seven-pound catalog of more than 80,000 individual supplies, from cleaning solvents to replacement engines, to find the products they needed and then call or fax the orders in, picking them up at one of the company's 500 stores, or waiting for delivery. In the early 1990s, Grainger started distributing the catalogs via CD-ROM—which made the searching faster, but didn't do much to speed up the actual order and delivery process.

Bielinski, a group vice president, was taken aback by the calls from the telcos, but he caught on fast: they figured they could skim off big bucks if they put Grainger's catalog online and got just a little slice of each transaction.

Nice try.

Once the telcos started putting the pieces together for him, Bielinski was inspired with a much bigger vision of how an Internet-based catalog could help Grainger's customers find what they wanted faster and get it delivered faster.

Grainger could create a platform for cross selling, customized selling and other strategies that he'd long wanted to try.

He got $5 million to launch what has turned out to be a company-transforming effort. By the time May 1999 rolled around, Grainger's online effort had escalated to a $50 million, 150-person division that extended far beyond a mere online catalog.

"It's totally driven by the rational habits of corporate buyers," explains Bielinski. Through OrderZone.com, FindMRO.com and other search and catalog functions, Grainger has created a completely dynamic pricing structure for the 220,000 items it offers.

"We realized that we had to keep track of **different prices negotiated on various products by different customers**," says Bielinski.

"Instead of seeing that as a pain, we decided to make that dynamic pricing backbone a critical competitive edge. **We'll build a custom catalog for any customer who wants it**, and that catalog reflects that company's negotiated prices (with Grainger)."

To tackle this gargantuan task, Bielinski knew that he would have to assemble even more resources than he had on tap at Grainger. He saw how fast Dell, IBM and Cisco were moving to dominate their markets, and, after using internal folks to develop a first site, he adopted the high tech firms' Biz Dev techniques to do the same for Grainger.

At first, Grainger tapped its internal resources to Internet-enable its catalog.

OrderZone.com was launched on June 7, 1999. It grouped together six of Grainger's biggest suppliers into a unified interactive one-stop shop so that customers of all sizes could order and track supplies from electrical parts to paper clips.

In April 1999, Grainger partnered with German software giant SAP AG to integrate Grainger's catalog with SAP's procurement software, making it easier for SAP customers to order through Grainger.

Then, in May and August 1999, Grainger partnered with CommerceOne and Intelisys Electronic Commerce, respectively, to use their procurement software as a platform that customers could use to speed up their internal procurement and purchase order process—which costs an estimated $150 per order. Leveraging Intelisys software engages Grainger more deeply with its customers' ordering processes, enmeshing those processes with the Grainger site.

Just three months later, Grainger was able to introduce FindMRO.com, a 'personal shopper' service that blends tools that customers use to evaluate the specifications of infrequently required items, then match those specifications with the appropriate items offered by Grainger suppliers. That concept paved the way for a ten-year agreement to manage an expected $300 million worth of procurement for B.F. Goodrich.

Grainger's momentum continued as it partnered with Fairmarkets to introduce an auction site in November 1999 (for discontinued items), and in January 2000, teamed up with Ace Hardware Corp. to link FindMRO.com to its ACENET site..

Then came TotalMRO.com, an infrastructure that gives corporate users completely real-time access to product availability, pricing and other sourcing details. TotalMRO.com was put together with partners such as Ariba, BEA Systems, Requisite Technology, and WebMethods, as well as numerous suppliers that had already gone onto the Web.

Grainger continued to add distribution and marketing alliances with specialized marketplaces, such as ENI-Net.com (which serves the environmental industry), and manufacturers Black & Decker, DeWalt as participants in its auction site. By the end of 1999, Grainger's three online sites had processed sales of $102 million (an annualized rate of more than $200 million). Sales made online averaged $240, compared to $130 for offline sales.

By spring 2000, Grainger's commitment to Biz Dev had grown so strong that it created a whole team devoted solely to working with MRO product distributors and technology partners to come up with new structures for selling through the Internet. Based on its success with U.S. Internet users, Grainger announced its first international Web-based procurement partnership, with SK Global, for the Korean market.

The effort hasn't been without its bumps. Grainger spent so much on information technology in 1999—adding new internal systems as well as pushing ahead with its Internet services—that its fourth quarter 1999 earnings dropped by half, even though sales were up 7 percent. Still, Grainger met its goal of $160 million in online sales for the year 2000, a small but significant portion of its $4.3 billion in annual revenues.

"Especially for networks based on intellectual assets, the initial cost of establishing the relationships is great, but the ongoing cost is much smaller. To reap the benefits of a partnership, it's essential to stick with it so that you reach the profitable plateau."
—*Network to Net Worth*, Credit Suisse First Boston Corporation

One of Grainger's promises to its customers was to pass on the efficiencies it captured through online operations by driving down prices. Because it costs Grainger 4 percent less to process online transactions than those consummated over the phone or via fax, Grainger offers free freight on online orders.

Even customers can add up those results of Biz Dev.

Pretty soon, Grainger's customers will overcome the last hurdle: remembering that the company itself is "W.W. Grainger," not "www.grainger.com."

As you recognize more ways that your Biz Dev frontiersmen have cleared the way so that the rest of the company can settle in and start farming, you'll detect Biz Dev's true influence on all aspects of your company's growth, revenues and influence.

It does work. It works for Starbelly, and it will work for you. As the old economy and new economy blend into the E-conomy, Biz Dev will emerge ever more strongly as a clearly defined strategy—the best strategy for growing your company fast, straight and long.

Check it out

W. W. Grainger's site shows dozens of ways that their Biz Dev partnerships can help out their customers, at **http://my.grainger.com**

I like getting the lowdown on companies at Kiplinger's site, at **http://www.kiplinger.com**

For a lively, well-run brokerage built on Biz Dev, see Charles Schwab at **http://www. schwab.com**. For a stodgier and less Biz Dev approach, see Datek at **http://www.datek.com**

Take Biz Dev to the next level!
For other resources, ongoing conversation, and the BizDev3.0 newsletter, join us at **http://www.BizDev3.com**

Stop reading!

Time to stop reading, and get busy doing Biz Dev! But if you want a few takeaway points, here are some ideas that will help you triangulate what Biz Dev is, and why it's worth doing.

Biz Dev keeps your competitors off-balance

Alliances and partnerships in the Internet world keep competitors **off guard**, potential customers interested, and current customers feeling that they're part of an exciting rocket ride. Meanwhile, they let your company grow into its vision.

How many times have you seen a facet of potential in another company—a supplier, a vendor, even a competitor—that would enable you to serve your customers better, faster, if only you had it?

But you don't have it.

That other company has it. Instead of licensing that ability, or copying it, or pretending it isn't important, ally with it.

That **point of strength**, combined with yours, becomes a service or product uniquely valuable to your customer—what she needs, when she needs it.

She doesn't have time to wait for you to recreate the wheel. So don't. Use alliances and partnerships instead.

Biz Dev looks out for the customers' best interests

Let's say that one of those interests is precision. One customer might need a database management system expressly designed for managing targeted e-mail offers that will be broadcast to small businesses based on their customer profiles, which are stored in the customer's own database.

Does she want to listen to a dozen salespeople reel through a pitch about databases in general? Or the many wonderful uses of e-mail as a marketing tool? No.

Does she want to explain all this to her company's internal, overworked IT team, which is already swamped with requests from marketing and trying to convert an old inventory management system to interface with the e-commerce order system? No, she does not want to burden them.

Yet, she wants to get her e-mail offers out to the businesses that have said they want them, and she wants to leave the businesses that don't want them alone.

If you were that customer's Web developer, and you knew of her problem, it wouldn't help her if you stayed quiet. If you knew of a company that offered a reliable, flexible, high quality e-mail database management system, you'd tell her. Of course you would.

Biz Dev Buzz: The better you know your customers, the more Biz Dev opportunities you perceive.

Lead the crowd

Winning goodwill by making a referral used to be enough. It's one way to guarantee that you'll get at least a couple of thank-you fruitcakes every Christmas.

But that kind of generosity is not enough any more. When you have a Biz Dev mindset, you say to yourself, "If this customer has that problem, others do, too. And if others do, there's an opportunity for me to enhance my reputation as a total-solutions guy, to work out a regular deal with a supplier that helps me by helping my customer. I refer to him, he refers to me. We both win."

You **both win** because you have both precisely targeted that customer's need. You didn't try to sell her something she didn't need. You didn't tell her that she didn't **have** a need. You didn't build a half-baked, jerry-rigged system.

You found a way to align existing market resources to meet that precise need. If she has another need, that e-mail database management firm probably won't be able to fulfill it. That's OK. You can help your client find another of your allies who **can** fill that new need.

These hunches are time sensitive. They fade. Your clairvoyant perception of your customer's need becomes more irrelevant as time passes. If you dismissed her urgency to get a database up and running so that she could electronically address and blast out those promotional e-mails, you'd missed the opportunity entirely.

The first one to the starting line wins

Speed matters. **The faster you respond to a customer's need, the more likely you are to gain that customer's trust, loyalty and continued business.** Any competitors who see you hesitate will quickly seize on that crucial flaw. They will ramp up their timing to deliver critical help to your potential customers just a step before you do. Because they are there first, they will appear to be more caring, to have a better understanding of the essence of the problem that needs to be solved.

Even if you are barely edged out, you will be the copycat, the also-ran. Of course, the guy who gets there first can still blow it. He might misunderstand the customer's problem and get there first, with the wrong solution. He might oversell what he is offering. His speed may backfire on him if he delivers the wrong solution, first. Then, you have a chance to recapture the initiative. Still, counting on someone else to make a mistake is a poor substitute for understanding the customer's urgency to get the problem solved, and matching that urgency with the right solution, promptly offered.

You can be there first, with the right solution, by aligning yourself with another company that also understands how important it is to respond to customers when they actually need a problem solved, not before, and not after. Successful business development finds allies who aren't afraid to use the accelerator to get to the finish line first. **If it's important to your customer, it's important to your allies.**

Biz Dev Buzz: Grow your company fastest and best by internalizing the Web model, to reach out and grab the relevant bits from the best of what's out there, combine it with your best, and deliver it to customers, immediately.

Better fast and imperfect than perfect and irrelevant

When you see a market opportunity, you must act to Biz Dev it.

Act means act. It doesn't mean study, report, analyze, examine, think about, confer, meet about or discuss.

Much of that kind of pondering is valuable, but—and here's the crucial difference—all that internal analyzing and research must happen **at the same time** that you are acting. If you study, report, analyze, and so on, and *then* act, your opportunity will be gone. Swifter competitors will have moved, or the problem may have been solved in another way, or the customers may have simply decided the heck with it, they had bigger problems to solve and they don't care anymore about that particular one.

Of course, analysis is valuable. But if you are truly operating within your company's own core competencies, you will already know how to get going on developing this product.

Here's how it can work: your engineers can be designing at the same time the distribution folks are figuring out how to get the product shipped, and the supply specialists are locating the best components, and the marketing folks are busy getting that snappy name ready—all in parallel.

Yes, you'll have to jostle around and make lots of adjustments amongst each other's functions as you get closer to rollout. Some effort will be lost, ditched along the way as market insight starts to roll in to refine the product even as it's being created. You may think of a better slogan after the product is introduced. That's the way it goes. You're not aiming at perfection, but immediate relevance.

Ride on fast coattails

Drawing in allies who understand the need to move quickly can make you fast. When you call your Biz Dev cohort at a partner company and she sees the same opportunity, the same way, just ten minutes into your conversation, you've added another engine to power your rollout. Her company's strengths become your company's strengths.

By adopting what they're good at and adding that to what your company is already good at, you're free to create what doesn't yet exist. That might be a targeted twist to an existing product: for instance, we tailor our StarStores to the particular needs of sponsoring companies, reflecting their own preferences for product mix. We're replacing their former methods of selling logo and customized merchandise.

An ally has to have horsepower, too. **The company you partner with must do what it does extremely well.** You are borrowing its core strengths on behalf of your mutual customers. A company that claims to have the capacity to customize that e-mail marketing database in a month had better be able to do it. If it fails, you do too, at least as far as that customer is concerned. Instead of 1+1=3 in credibility, you will suffer from 1-1=-3 credibility.

The fast-forward evolution of e-commerce demands that companies deliver products and services to market in weeks, not months or even years.

When you ally your company with others that have complementary strengths, you free up your company to intensify its efforts to create and deliver its own products fast. That makes you an attractive ally to others. **Effective Biz Dev funnels resources to wherever they can be most efficiently used.** Your internal capital is concentrated on creating the best, deepest, richest, most useful and valuable service and product. Meanwhile, you are tapping into the best, deepest, richest, most useful and valuable services and products offered by other companies.

Superficial 'partnerships' fool no one. Biz Dev success is not weighted by pure partner poundage. A supplier may be a partner if it actually works with your product development team to deliver materials specifically for products geared for your customers. But a supplier who delivers fifty pounds of coffee to your offices every week is unlikely to be a partner, even if your product team can only get your product to market if they are marinating in caffeine.

A supplier becomes a partner when you share the risks in targeting a new market together, developing a product or service that neither of you could offer individually.

Your customers are counting on you to know your segment of the market better than anyone else.

When you ally yourself with another company, that new partner is benefiting from the credibility that you have carefully developed with your customers. Your customers know you. They believe you. They will believe in the alliance if you say so. So make sure that your partner has the resources to deliver on the promise that they make to you to jointly develop or introduce a product. **You can't have your partner's shoddy work invalidating the trust that your customers have in you.**

Partnerships must be immediately relevant

The essence of Biz Dev is to find that **critical touchpoint** where you and your potential partner add value to each other's mutual markets. One touchpoint, for one market.

I'm not talking about an old-style partnership in which you're trading classified secrets and patented formulas. In Biz Dev, you're deciding to pool your strengths to reach one market, from one perspective, at one point in time.

The simpler the proposition, the more quickly everyone else involved will see the value it offers.

That's important for drawing in others in your company to make the alliance a reality, but it's even more important for communicating with customers.

If customers won't instantaneously grasp the value that the proposition brings to them, don't bother. It has to be a single crystalline idea that sheds light on one element of their own operation.

- "Same day delivery"
- "Real-time chat to help customers shop at your online store"
- "Database management"
- "Instant real-time tracking of your order as it's being shipped"
- "Real-time inventory availability"

It takes no leap of faith to see the benefits of these concepts. They're plain and simple, as are all successful Biz Dev alliances.

Your partner is your customer's partner

Customers crave understanding. They need to know that you understand their business and what they're trying to accomplish. They want proof that you're helping them get there. When you arrange allies and partners that help you help them, you're not just communicating that you're a hot business with lots of contacts (or VC capital).

You're conveying your purpose: **you're saying that because the service you offer is vitally important to your customers, you're moving heaven and earth to deliver that service to them.** You're pulling together the best resources you can to deliver that value to your customers—right away.

How promptly you do this is a key part of your marketing message. It's who you are to your customers: the company that anticipated their need and created a product out of thin air to meet that need.

It doesn't matter to the customer that the product is partially developed by your own engineers and product development team, and partially the result of other companies' strengths. What does matter to your customer is that it is up, running, and helping her accomplish her own goal.

You can agree with her that it's not perfect. Believe me, she'll help you understand **her** definition of perfection. As long as she knows that you're committed to integrating customer feedback, and anticipating customer needs, and improving that service continually, she knows this: that you and she are pulling together to make her life easier, and her company's functions smoother, more profitable and more responsive to its markets.

Biz Dev Buzz: The way your company manages Biz Dev becomes part of your overall corporate image.

Speak loudly and carry a big stick

Grabbing the attention of the market is critical.

While not all alliances are exclusive, the combination of your own skills with those of your partner **can be** an exclusive proposition for your mutual customers. Your partnership signals to your market that your new product or service is on the way.

Customers may hesitate to buy something else because they want to see what your alliance produces.

And you have, temporarily at least, **stymied** your competitors. They may have had that idea, but they weren't as quick as you. In their hesitation, they lost.

Even if their announcement is a day later, it's still a day too late to be first. You have captured the position of the one to beat.

And, in fact, you **could** be beat, if you don't keep on moving quickly with new alliances, promptly followed up with enough actual product and service deliveries to build credibility, draw and retain customers, and, oh yeah, bring in money. Believe me, nobody would be impressed if we announced that we were revolutionizing the way organizations manage the whole process of designing and buying custom apparel and merchandise, and then never shipped a single shirt.

Biz Dev is not the Chamber of Commerce Networking Breakfast at warp speed. Only companies that offer the right product, service, or expertise, **and** that match your own company's sense of speed to market, can be real partners. You don't want to hold up your partners, or be held back by them. You don't want to be shackled to a company that says it understands the needs of your mutual customers, yet somehow never quite achieves preeminence in any of its product lines.

Start now

In a way, Biz Dev reflects the hothouse economic atmosphere surrounding Silicon Valley. In the Valley, nearly every employee has worked somewhere else and everybody knows someone at another company. Most employees have a pretty good idea what other companies are hatching. Consultants, bankers and suppliers move freely among companies of all sizes. There are few secrets. **This is the cultural milieu that spawned Biz Dev—a culture of openness, expectation of rapid change, and a constant search for the next Great Idea.**

Your company must devote internal resources to Biz Dev so that you can catch and leverage your own next Great Idea. If that means changing your company's culture to involve everyone, from the greenest customer service rep to the CEO, in looking for potential alliances, then you must dig in to **create that culture.** If it means throwing the old organizational chart out the window, then let it fly. If it means that the product development teams must constantly reorganize and reform to get products to incorporate your allies' strengths into your own new products, then that's how it must be.

Regardless of your industry or your company, you can be a Biz Dev advocate if you develop the mindset. Pick up the phone. Introduce yourself. Ask to speak to the person in charge of business development. If that doesn't work, try the CEO. CEOs in most small to mid-sized companies these days don't hide behind layers of minions—it's relatively easy to make a pitch. Just make it focused and fast. Work under the assumption that you know everybody at every company—after all, it only takes a few minutes on the phone to meet and find just about anyone you want.

If this sounds like sales, you're on the right track. The glad-ta-meetcha aspect of Biz Dev is very much like sales. But Biz Dev rolls up elements of sales, marketing, and business forecasting along with personal characteristics of leadership, fearlessness and a certain prophetic ability to perceive new value emerging from fresh combinations of already existing services and products. You never know when someone's crazy idea will suddenly start to make sense as the market catches up to his prognostication. You never know when an acquaintance will land a great job at a hot start-up, or, just as valuable, in a market-making position at a profitable traditional company.

As a Biz Dev specialist you see this with the perception of a clairvoyant. To you, it's so simple: our service to this customer would be enhanced if we could add "X." This other company has "X," so let's approach them to see how, together, we can each expand our markets and services by putting together our "Y" with their "X." Together, we'll present this to our target market. We'll hold hands for this deal. If it works, we'll keep holding hands, or maybe add other ways to hold hands. If it doesn't work, well, at least we've told our market that we're willing to take risks to come up with better ways to serve them.

Before long, you've got a good idea as to who's on the same wavelength. You see the needs of your mutual markets in the same way. You both have a working appreciation for the simple, lucid concept that can be enacted immediately. You both detest drawn out decision-making processes that take so long that the market opportunity is lost because you've been stuck in so many feasibility reviews.

Congratulations! You've found a partner.

It's time to cut your first deal. Make sure you stop by at **www.BizDev3.com** to tell us how it goes!

Biz Dev Buzz: Be bold! Just get out there and start looking for opportunities and suggesting your ideas to Biz Dev gurus at other companies.

Check it out

If you can't stop reading, here are some books that will inspire you, starting with two by Seth Godin, who wrote our foreword.

Permission Marketing: Turning Strangers into Friends, and Friends into Customers by Seth Godin and Don Peppers (Simon & Schuster, 1999). Fantastic book, must read.

Unleashing the Ideavirus by Seth Godin, Malcolm Gladwell (Foreword) (Do You Zoom, 2000). What a great idea!

Blown to Bits: How the New Economics of Information Transforms Strategy by Philip Evans, Thomas S. Wurster (Harvard Business School, 1999). Good detail on the E-conomy.

Competitive Intelligence: How to Gather, Analyze, and Use Information to Move Your Business to the Top by Larry Kahaner (Touchstone Books, 1998). Nice overview, with plenty of good introductory material for beginners.

Faster: The Acceleration of Just About Everything by James Gleick (Pantheon, 1999). A tour of high speed.

Loyalty.com: Customer Relationship Management in the New Era of Internet Marketing by Frederick Newell (McGraw-Hill, 2000). Biz Dev meets the Rolodex.

New Rules for the New Economy: 10 Radical Strategies for a Connected World by Kevin Kelly (Penguin, 1999). Complexity theory applied to the E-conomy.

The Cluetrain Manifesto: The End of Business As Usual by Christopher Locke, Rick Levine, Doc Searls, David Weinberger (Perseus, 2000). Get a clue and ride it.

Take Biz Dev to the next level!

For other resources, ongoing conversation, and the BizDev3.0 newsletter, join us at **http://www.BizDev3.com**

NOTES

Introduction

Daly, James, "Howdy Partner," *Business 2.0* (Dec. 26, 2000).

Opening up Biz Dev

"E-Business Survey by PwC and The Conference Board Finds Global Corporations Having to Make Up Lost Ground in Digital Economy," PriceWaterhouseCoopers (March 21, 2000).

Step 1

Hamel, Gary, "Reinvent Your Company," *Fortune*, vol. 141, no. 12 (June 12, 2000).
Network to Net Worth—Exploring Network Dynamics, Credit Suisse First Boston Corporation Equity Research (May 11, 2000).

Step 2

Kelly, Kevin, *New Rules for the New Economy: 10 Radical Strategies for a Connected World*, p. 46 (Penguin USA, 1999).
Ibid.
Byrne, John A., "The 21st Century Corporation," *Business Week* (Aug. 21-28, 2000).

Step 3

Tapscott, Don, David Ticoll, and Alex Lowy, *Digital Capital: Harnessing the Power of Business Webs*, p. 6 (Harvard Business School Press, 2000).
Gleick, James, *Faster: The Acceleration of Just About Anything*, p. 76 (Vintage Books, 2000).
Kelly, Kevin, *New Rules for the New Economy: 10 Radical Strategies for a Connected World*, p. 118 (Penguin USA, 1999).
"US Internet Trade Soars to $6 Trillion in 2005, Businesses Must Invest in Multiple Selling Models or Risk Market Share," Jupiter Communications (June 26, 2000).
"E-Business Survey by PwC and The Conference Board Finds Global Corporations Having to Make Up Lost Ground in Digital Economy," PriceWaterhouseCoopers (March 21, 2000).
Gleick, p. 51.
Ibid., p. 41.

Step 4

Network to Net Worth—Exploring Network Dynamics, Credit Suisse First Boston Corporation Equity Research (May 11, 2000).
"Weekly Statistical Summary," *eMarketer* (April 24, 2000).

Step 5

Kelly, Kevin, *New Rules for the New Economy: 10 Radical Strategies for a Connected World*, p. 137 (Penguin USA, 1999).

Evans, Thomas, and Thomas Wurster, *Blown to Bits: How the New Economics of Information Transforms Strategy*, p. 220 (Harvard Business School Press, 1999).

Aspatore, Jonathan R., *Digital Rush: Nine Internet Start-Ups In the Race for Dot.Com Riches*, p. 265 (AMACOM, 2000).

Ibid.

Fabris, Peter, "Getting Together," *CIO Magazine* (Dec. 15, 1998/Jan. 1, 1999) (Harbor Research).

Step 6

Anders, George, "Honesty is the Best Policy—Trust Us," *Fast Company*, issue 37, p. 262 (August 2000).

Patsuris, Penelope, "The ABCs of ASPs," Forbes.com (July 17, 2000).

Network to Net Worth—Exploring Network Dynamics, Credit Suisse First Boston Corporation Equity Research (May 11, 2000).

Nordstrom, Kjell, and Jonas Ridderstrale, *Funky Business: Talent Makes Capital Dance*, p. 167 (Financial Times Prentice Hall Publishing, 2000).

Step 7

Harbison, John, and Peter Pekar, Jr., *Smart Alliances: A Practical Guide to Repeatable Success* (Jossey-Bass, 1998) (http://www.bah.com/viewpoints/smart-alliances.html).

Kelly, Kevin, *New Rules for the New Economy: 10 Radical Strategies for a Connected World*, p. 47 (Penguin USA, 1999).

Fabris, Peter, "Getting Together," *CIO Magazine* (Dec. 15, 1998/Jan. 1, 1999) (Booz Allen information).

Kelly, p. 116.

"The Internet Company Handbook–v. 2.0," Morgan Stanley Dean Witter Equity Research (June 2000).

Kelly, p. 116.

Schrage, Michael, and Tom Peters, *Serious Play: How the World's Best Companies Simulate to Innovate*, p. 1 (Harvard Business School Press, 1999).

Step 8

Peters, Tom, "Lessons in Leadership," Tom Peters SeminarM3, St. Louis, Mo. (Jan. 24, 2001).

Michaels, Ed, "The War for Talent," McKinsey & Co. (1998).

Step 9

Harbison, John, and Peter Pekar, Jr., *Smart Alliances: A Practical Guide to Repeatable Success* (Jossey-Bass, 1998) (http://www.bah.com/viewpoints/smart-alliances.html).

Network to Net Worth—Exploring Network Dynamics, Credit Suisse First Boston Corporation Equity Research (May 11, 2000).

INDEX